Accession no.
00936135

WITHDRAWN

KNOWING LANDSCAPE

Parks
and Gardens

LLED
D
LED

ED

KNOW THE LANDSCAPE

Parks
and Gardens

Anthea Taigel
Tom Williamson

CHESTER COLLEGE

ACC. No.
00936135

DEPT.

CLASS No.
712.60942   TAI

LIBRARY

B.T. BATSFORD LTD · LONDON

© Anthea Taigel and Tom Williamson 1993

First published 1993

All rights reserved. No part of this publication may be reproduced, in any form or by any means, without permission from the Publisher

Typeset by Best-set Typesetter Ltd, Hong Kong
and printed in Great Britain by
The Bath Press, Avon

Published by B.T. Batsford Ltd
4 Fitzhardinge Street, London W1H 0AH

A CIP catalogue record for this book is
available from the British Library

ISBN 0 7134 6728 2

Contents

Illustrations

Acknowledgements

This book would not have been possible without the advice, information and encouragement received from a large number of people. We would like to thank colleagues and friends at the Centre of East Anglian Studies, especially Jon Finch, Susanna Wade Martins, A. Hassell Smith, David Brown, Linda Campbell and Kate Skipper. Thanks also to Beverley Peters; Jane Harding; Barry Doyle; Robin Watson; Tom McGeary; T.R. Cubitt; Paul Farrow; Judith Cooke; Tim Stanger; Mike Ball; Jean Williamson; Lord Ferrers; Judith Cantell; Liz Bellamy; Roger Taigel; Jon Phibbs; Liz Atcheson; Captain W.H. Bulwer-Long; the Marquess of Cholmondeley; John Dean; Paul Rutledge; Martin Wainwright; John Dixon Hunt; and Chris Taylor. We would also like to thank the staff of the following institutions for their help and patience: North Yorkshire Record Office, Northallerton; West Country Studies Department, County Library, Exeter; Devon Record Office, Exeter; Somerset Record Office, Taunton; Norfolk Record Office, Norwich; Local Studies Library, Norwich; Berkshire Record Office, Reading; Hertfordshire Record Office, Hertford; Buckinghamshire Record Office, Aylesbury; East Suffolk Record Office, Ipswich; Cambridge University Library; Southwark Local Studies Library; the John Innes Foundation; and the Halifax Local Studies Library.

Special thanks to the following for permission to reproduce photographs or archive material. Norfolk Record Office (Figs 1 and 3); Brian Horne (4 and 18); Richard Muir (5); Cambridge Committee for Aerial Photography (6, 13, 21 and 32); East Suffolk Record Office (16); Castle Museum, Norwich (20); Country Life (26); Cambridge University Library (2 and 30); Hertfordshire Record Office (31); Buckinghamshire Record Office (34); The Science Museum, London (45); National Monuments Record (10, 54, 75); Derek Edwards (Norfolk Landscape Archaeology) (52); the Bridewell Museum, Norwich (53 and 58); Northallerton Record Office (8 and 23); Roger Taigel (66); Halifax Library (Local Studies Department) (67); James Morris and the Landmark Trust (79); Alan Robertson and Southwark Local Studies Library (71).

For a wider discussion of estates the reader is referred to another volume in this series: *Estates and the English Countryside* by J.H. Bettey (1993).

Preface

The English countryside today bears witness to centuries of human activity and interference in numerous ways that can be interpreted by the informed observer using the skills of the archaeologist and the local historian. This new, wide-ranging series looks at the development of the landscape in Britain and examines the forces at work which have shaped its changing appearance from prehistoric times to the present day.

Each book takes a characteristic aspect of the landscape – such as estates, monasteries, roads, canals and railways, traces its history and development, explains its function and studies its impact on the landscape throughout history. The subjects are popular and may have easily recognizable features that can still be visited and enjoyed, but some of the effects they have had on the landscape of today are subtle and unexpected and their influence has profoundly changed the look of the countryside around us.

For instance, castles and manor houses are still visible, but so too, to the trained eye, are their fishponds and kitchen gardens, long since demolished or destroyed above ground. What are the reasons behind barely discernible ditches and banks; why is an ancient track just where it is; why were certain villages deserted; less obviously, even why are some trees shaped the way they are? These are some of the intriguing questions discussed in this series.

The authors show how the techniques of landscape research can be used by anyone to enable them to recognize and decipher the signs of various periods of the human past in their own environment. They also guide the reader to some of the sources of documentary evidence and point out particular areas of research that can still be pursued, enabling the individual to make a real contribution.

The series builds up to present a new insight into familiar views and landscapes and brings out some of the hidden features of the British countryside.

Studying gardens

Garden, society, landscape

This book is about the history of parks and gardens in England, and in particular about the large landscapes laid out around country houses in the eighteenth and nineteenth centuries. The reader may be wondering why another book on the history of gardens is necessary, for there are many good accounts already in print. The reason is simple. Most are written from the perspective of the art historian, rather than from that of the social historian or the archaeologist. They are, therefore, concerned with different kinds of issues than those which interest the historian of the landscape. Such books dwell on the life and works of famous designers like William Kent, Humphry Repton or Lancelot 'Capability' Brown, and on the philosophical and aesthetic notions which supposedly influenced their work. This is perfectly reasonable, as far as it goes, but it is only part of the story. Abstract ideas were only one factor influencing the design of gardens. The grounds of the country house had to be lived in and used, and the lifestyle and resources of the owner, his attitudes to family, friends, allies and neighbours, were all of vital importance in shaping the structure of parks. Gardens were not just 'art'. Their form was moulded by all aspects of the lives of their creators, not just by the views of the verbose writers whose texts cluttered up the shelves of a gentleman's study.

The art-historical perspective has another drawback. In most books, gardens seem to be removed from economic and environmental concerns. There is little impression that they existed in a real world, not just in the realm of art and ideas; a world in which money and land had to be found for their creation and maintenance, and in which both the previous landscape, and the surrounding one, offered possibilities and imposed limitations on the execution of a design. There is, in addition, little sense that gardens developed over time, almost always incorporating and adapting features from earlier phases. Gardens, like vernacular buildings, have histories, not 'dates', and even the 'great names' like Brown were usually adapting and updating layouts created by earlier designers, rather than creating 'works of art' on an empty canvas.

There is a further problem. Most books on garden history concentrate on what happened at a handful of 'important' gardens, like Stowe, Rousham or Chatsworth; gardens which were frequently visited, written about or illustrated by contemporaries. Such places were, however, famous precisely because they were particularly grand, new or unusual, *not* because they were normal or commonplace. They were also, for the most part, the gardens and parks of the greatest landowners, men of national importance, with estates of 10,000 acres or more. And so, in reality, the history of gardens, as usually recounted, is the history of the pleasure grounds created by the super-rich or the super-famous. These great layouts are important, and will be discussed here at some length, partly because they were very influential in the development of garden fashions, but also because they have, often by virtue of their scale, an immense impact on the modern landscape. It must, however, be remembered that the lifestyles, finances and interests of their owners often had little in common with those of the broad mass of the local gentry.

In order to obtain a clearer idea about how parks and gardens developed in England, we urgently need to find out about a greater number, and a much larger range, of sites. Such work is now being carried out by a number of people and institutions, all over the country, but it is still in its early stages. There is a vast number of gardens in England, and also considerable regional variations in the way in which they developed, and so the task is an immense one. The study of designed landscapes is a useful, and immensely enjoyable, field for the local historian and amateur archaeologist. It is for this reason, but also to indicate the kinds of evidence on which the rest of the arguments in this book are based, that we begin with a brief description of the sources which can be used to study the history of parks and gardens.

Maps, plans and illustrations

Maps, plans and illustrations, whether in published form, in the private archives of country houses or lodged in County Record Offices, are perhaps the most important sources of evidence for the garden historian. Almost all of them can be of some value, providing their particular limitations are recognized and respected.

Until the advent of the large-scale Ordnance Survey maps at the end of the nineteenth century, the most detailed surveys were estate maps, that is, privately commissioned manuscript maps produced for a wide variety of purposes. These are usually dated, and often carry the surveyor's name. Some were intended for display, to hang on the walls of a gentleman's chamber or study, and these were, accordingly, intricately coloured and detailed. Most estate maps are accurate within the limits of the surveyor's competence and equipment. They often had to be, since one of their uses was for the sale or exchange of land. A dispute over land measured in a 1738 survey held up the transfer of the Havcringland estate in Norfolk in the 1770s for almost three years. This survey ultimately proved to be inaccurate in its measurement of a single field, and the vendor had to pay compensation. Such mistakes could cost a surveyor his livelihood, and had to be avoided at all costs.[1] Yet while such maps might be accurate in the features they depict, this does not mean that they necessarily show everything that was present in the landscape at the time. Maps were made for a purpose, and if the depiction of a certain feature was irrelevant to this, then it was omitted. It is, therefore, impossible to argue that because a clump or pond is not shown on a map of a certain date it did not exist at this time.

Tithe Award maps, which were mostly produced between 1836 and 1841, are another important source of information. They exist for many thousands of parishes, especially in the south-east and west of England. They were produced as part of the process by which tithes were commuted from payments in kind to a statutory rental imposed on land. The tithes due from any area were related to the way in which it was used: the rates imposed on woodland, arable, pasture, etc. were all different and we can, therefore, be confident that the boundaries of areas with different land uses, or in different ownership, will be shown with some accuracy. The limitation of these maps, however, lies in their often cavalier treatment of the (to the tithe surveyors) irrelevant finer details of parks and pleasure grounds. Thus, for example, the precise disposition of trees in a park, or the patterns of walks or flower beds in a pleasure ground, were of no interest, and if shown at all were usually drawn in a somewhat schematic fashion. Once again, therefore, we cannot argue from negative evidence: the omission of an avenue from a Tithe Award map does not imply that it did not exist at the time. What is more serious, however, is that some of these maps show garden features which had already ceased to exist at the time the survey was made. This is because, while detailed guidelines were laid down for the production of Tithe Award maps, and only those which conformed were scaled as 'First Class', many fell short of the ideal.[2] Where there were few owners in a parish, and where the commutation of the tithes was, therefore, a fairly straightforward affair, an existing estate map might be used for the definition of the tithable areas. This might show the details of pleasure grounds as they had existed 20 or even 30 years before the date of commutation.

Enclosure maps – the surveys made to accompany the Parliamentary enclosure of open fields and commons in the eighteenth and early nineteenth centuries – also exist for many parishes. These often indicate the external boundaries of parks, but seldom their internal details. These maps were mainly concerned with the areas to be enclosed, and with the new landscape which was to replace them.[3]

Enclosure maps were concerned with very major alterations to the structure of the landscape. Another type of map, again dating from the late eighteenth and nineteenth centuries, was produced to accompany more limited changes. Until 1773, public rights of way could only be

closed or moved by calling a writ of *ad quod damnum* in the court of Chancery, or by passing a bill in Parliament. Both of these were fairly expensive, cumbersome and time-consuming procedures. After 1773, however, changes to the road network could be made much more easily, by the use of Road Closure Orders. Alterations to minor roads simply had to be agreed by two presiding magistrates. The Road Order document registering these changes was accompanied by a (sometimes very sketchy) map, showing the line of the road or path affected, and that of any proposed replacement (Fig. 1). One of the main reasons why roads or paths were moved or terminated was to allow for the creation or expansion of a landscape park. The existence

1 *A Road Order Map relating to the closure of roads in Barwick (Norfolk), in 1792.*

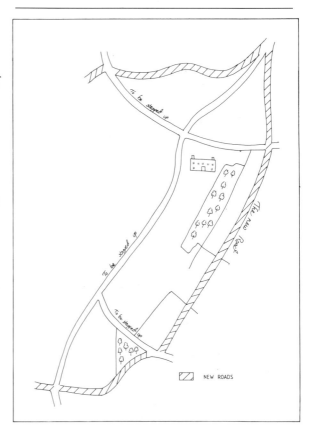

NEW ROADS

of a Road Order can, therefore, help to pin-point the date at which parks were created, or expanded, although in some cases, of course, this might lag some years behind the removal of the road in question. In addition, Road Order maps sometimes depict entrances, lodges, avenues and the existing boundaries of a park, where this served to identify the line of a road to be closed, or its replacement.

The maps so far discussed cover comparatively small areas: parts of a parish, a whole parish, or occasionally – in the case of some estate maps – groups of contiguous parishes. But from the sixteenth century onwards, maps showing much wider areas, and in particular whole counties, were also produced. County maps made before the last decades of the eighteenth century are of limited use to the garden historian. While they usually do show the location of parks, the cartographic convention employed for this purpose – a ring of paling – indicates that their surveyors were mainly concerned with deer parks. Landscape parks without deer, which were emerging in some numbers during the eighteenth century, were very unevenly depicted. From the 1770s, however, more detailed county surveys, often produced at a scale of 1in or

2   *William Faden's map of Gloucestershire, 1786: this is typical of later eighteenth-century maps in its depiction of landscape parks.*

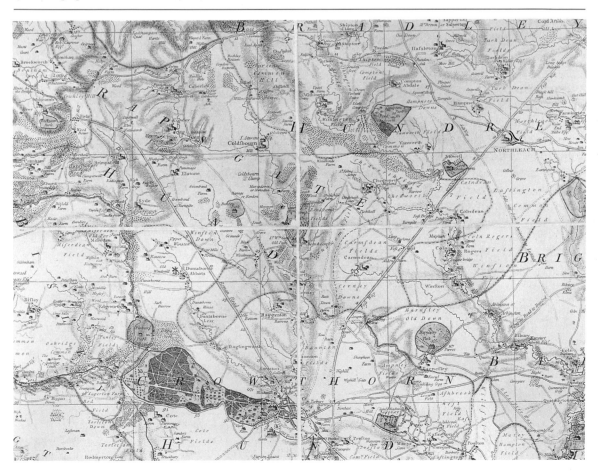

2in to the mile, appeared. These usually show the outline, and in many cases the main internal features, of parks and pleasure grounds (Fig. 2).

The last decades of the eighteenth century saw the first co-ordinated survey of the country, something which ultimately changed the entire face of cartography in England. Originally undertaken by the military establishment (hence the name 'Ordnance' Survey), the initial draught, at a scale of 2in to the mile, was far from accurate. In many instances surveyors plotted the principal settlements, boundaries and roads and filled in many other details (such as field boundaries) from their imagination. Perhaps because of such inaccuracies the survey, which continued into the 1810s, was not immediately published. Copies of the surveyors' drawings can, however, be obtained from the British Library in London. Although too much reliance should not be placed on the finer details these maps depict, they seem to show the main features of landscape parks with reasonable accuracy. The survey was eventually published after further alterations and emendments, at the reduced scale of 1 inch to the mile, from the late 1830s; the particular date, like that of the original survey, varies from region to region. This and subsequent editions can provide much useful information about the development of parks, although the small scale does not allow for the depiction of finer details.

The later, larger-scale Ordnance Survey maps, produced around 1885 at 6in to the mile and 25in to the mile, are infinitely more useful. These show the layout of beds and paths in gardens, even in quite small urban gardens; the location of glasshouses; and even the position of individual trees, all to a high degree of accuracy. Both the first editions, and the subsequent revisions, are an invaluable aid to the study of gardens and parks. Not only do they make it possible to identify many of the changes which have

taken place over the last hundred years, they can also provide a useful standard scale to which other maps can be reduced for the effective comparison of a landscape at different points in time.

Maps and plans are unquestionably the most important source of information for the garden historian. But they are also, potentially, the most misleading.

Nothing is more common than for those who intend to build to consult many advisors, and to collect different plans, from which they suppose it possible to make one perfect whole.[4]

Repton was writing here about buildings, but what he says was just as true of landscapes. The existence of a design on paper is no guarantee that it was ever faithfully reproduced on the ground. Sometimes a plan was abandoned in its entirety, as too expensive or out of keeping with the owner's taste; sometimes it was only executed in part. Even when a design was approved in outline, changes were often made during the course of the work, as ideas for improvements occurred to owner or designer, or as unforeseen problems arose. While unexecuted proposals are of considerable interest in showing the kinds of landscapes owners might have created if circumstances had been different, it is nevertheless essential, for a proper understanding of a landscape's history, to distinguish plans showing unexecuted proposals from surveys showing the landscape as it actually existed. The status of a plan as a proposal is sometimes evident from the rather sketchy nature of the cartography; such plans frequently showed little consideration for the actual topography of a site, since the details could be added if the scheme was accepted. Conversely, actual surveys can often be distinguished from proposals by their more detailed measurement and depiction of features, especially of the estate farmland. Titles, too, can be significant; those beginning 'A survey

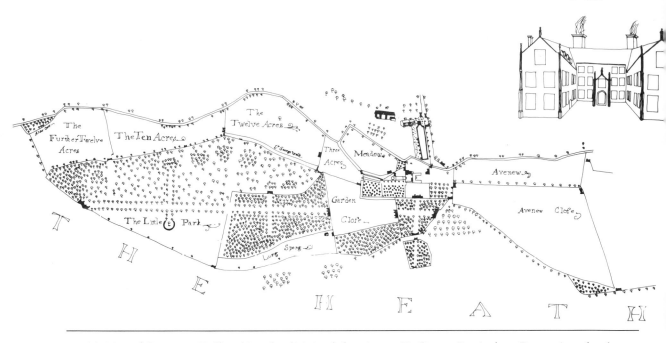

3 '*A Map of Costessey Hall and Lands adjoining belonging to Sir George Jerningham Baronet*': *undated, mid-eighteenth-century estate map from Norfolk.*

of the lands of . . .', were usually exactly what they said they were. The relationship of a map of uncertain status to other material in an estate archive is important. Thus, for example, the existence of several plans, by different surveyors, all dating from around the same time, must suggest that some were unexecuted proposals. Comparison with later plans, and with the landscape as it exists today, will often reveal the true nature of a map.

It might seem that the distinction between an 'accurate survey' and a 'design proposal' is, and was, fairly clear-cut. In reality, however, some maps and plans fall in between these two neat categories. Thus, for example, a survey of an estate made at the same time as the garden was undergoing major modifications might include both an accurate representation of the farmland, *and* a conjectural view of what the pleasure grounds might look like when completed. The extent of uncertainty and confusion which can lurk beneath the seemingly

'factual' surface of an estate map should never be underestimated. In March 1799 the surveyor John Bircham wrote a letter to William Earle Bulwer, of Heydon Hall in Norfolk:

I have this day begun the survey at Heydon. Hogden has been around with me and pointed out your instructions to him . . .

Bircham was to include details of:

The House Garden Buildings and Park . . . with the Ornamental Trees ponds etc leaving out all the fences which are intended to be thrown down & all the roads which are to be discontinued and lay out all the new Roads where they are intended to be and describe the Lodges intended to be built. . . . In short I presume you intend this should show the whole Premises as they will appear after the improvements are completed.[5]

This map does not survive. If it did, it would be a very confusing document, showing as it would Bircham's interpretation of Hogden's understanding of what Bulwer thought he *might* do. An extreme case perhaps, but not entirely atypical.

Illustrations also need to be treated with some care, for they, too, are only as good as the purpose for which they were intended. The choice of what was depicted, and how, can often be unrepresentative or misleading. Around 1700, a series of views of country houses was produced in a volume called *Britannia Illustrata* by Leonard Knyff and Johannes Kip. As with other contemporary depictions of country house landscapes, these are aerial perspectives; something which, in itself, should warn us against too credulous an acceptance of them as 'accurate representation' (Kip and Knyff did not go up in a balloon). In fact, it can be shown that their views often make the gardens appear far more extensive than they actually were. Given that *Britannia Illustrata* was funded by the subscriptions of landowners, it would be surprising if their houses and gardens were shown as *less* grand and imposing than they were in reality.

Indeed, most county histories and similar published works from the eighteenth century relied on subscriptions from the landed gentry. Illustrators were careful not to offend. Their view of a country seat was generally contrived to show the most fashionable or aesthetically pleasing areas of the landscape. So, for example, when landscape parks were the height of fashion, illustrators took care that their views did not include any surviving areas of walled gardens. The illustrations prepared by estate agents to accompany nineteenth-century sale catalogues also, needless to say, selected the most pleasing views of a house and its garden.

Rather more reliance can, perhaps, be placed on paintings or sketches that were privately commissioned although here, too, the house and landscape were obviously portrayed in the best possible light. And, as with maps, a painting might be commissioned prior to the completion of a new garden layout, so that the artist had to use his imagination to show the scene in maturity. Finally, we should always be aware that illustrations and plans could be used, in whole or part, as the basis for much later landscape schemes. When, in the nineteenth century, it became fashionable to recreate the formal gardens of an earlier age, these were sometimes based directly on illustrations hanging on the walls of a country house. Where a geometric garden exists today which closely resembles that shown on a painting of, say, the seventeenth century, the researcher should tread warily. It may, in reality, be largely or entirely a recreation of the nineteenth century.

Documentary sources

Illustrations, and in particular maps, are a vital source of information. But a vast amount can also be learnt from a wide variety of documents deposited in record offices or still remaining in private hands. Estate accounts – recording the payments made for goods, labour and services – are a good place to start. They frequently contain useful information about the creation or maintenance of a garden and also about payments made to gardeners and labourers, about the purchase of trees and flowers, about the construction of walls, terraces, greenhouses, and much more. But estates in the seventeenth, eighteenth and nineteenth centuries had a variety of ways of ordering their accounts, and there is also much variation in the survival of these documents. For some estates, separate accounts for the garden, or the park, have survived; and many have separate ledgers detailing the wood and timber planted in, and harvested from, the park and wider estate lands. For a few places, detailed day labour accounts exist, recording the day-by-day payments made to the labourers for a wide range of tasks: we can see them weeding the flower beds, levelling molehills in the park, planting new clumps and belts. At the other extreme, some estates – even very large ones – have no surviving accounts at all. They were all thrown away decades ago, together with other estate documents, and burnt on a bonfire in an attempt to tidy up the estate office.

Where copious archives have survived, all kinds of relevant material can come to light in the boxes and bundles. Bills for the purchase of plants and trees, estimates for the construction of lakes and garden buildings, and – especially from the late seventeenth and early eighteenth centuries – contracts made with gardeners for maintaining the garden. Thus, for example, at Stow Hall in Norfolk in 1692 Robert White, 'Town and Country Gardener', made a contract with Sir Thomas Hare, by which he agreed to:

. . . sufficiently maintaine and keep all and every the gardens, courtyards, orchards and walks of or belonging to Stow Hall . . . maintain and keep and furnish ye aforesaid house . . . with all necessary and sufficient kitchen garden stuff and also raise, inlay, graft and plant, as well all sorts of wallfruit, vines and other fruit, as also all sortes of greens (as the climit will allow), Pinks, Tulips, and other flowers and shall remove and set ye same in such places in ye gardens, courtyards, orchards, and walkes as ye said Sir Thomas Hare or his agent shall from time to time order.[6]

Sometimes lists of 'plants wanting for the garden' can be found, especially from the eighteenth century. Again at Stow, twenty years later, such a document lists, among other things lacking,

the plants for the quarters of the wildeness, 14 pears, 14 apples, 14 plums, 7 cherries all for standard trees. And for the Hedges round the quarters there is wanting 250 Yews, 230 Fellreys, 2 hundred Horenben, and for the edges of the borders by the gravel walks, there is wanting 2000 yeards of boxe . . .[7]

– a tantalizing description which casts a shaft of light on the otherwise obscure early history of an important garden.

Letters can also yield much information. Those concerned with estate administration – sent by the steward or agent to the owner, or vice versa – often provide important details of changes to the landscape being contemplated or carried out. Personal letters might discuss an owner's plans for a garden, the pleasures he or she derived from it, or the way it was used. The trouble with correspondence, however, is that much is uncatalogued, or is described in the index of an archive in only the vaguest terms. The researcher can, therefore, spend literally weeks thumbing through letters (often difficult to read) and yet glean only scraps of information, about the poor growth of the onions, or the damaged state of a melon on its arrival at the owner's town house in London. Much more useful are diaries and 'memoranda books' – that is, unorganized jottings concerning estate administration. These sources record purchases of trees and seed, changes made to the gardens, and also – once again – how the gardens were actually used by their owner. Diaries also contain information about other people's gardens, for in the eighteenth and nineteenth centuries it was common practice to visit not only the homes of friends and relations, but also other residences. Visits to country houses were not an invention of the twentieth century, and in the eighteenth and nineteenth centuries admission was usually granted to anyone who appeared sufficiently 'respectable', in return for an appropriate tip to the gardener or housekeeper. Some gardens were visited so frequently that arrangements were more organized. At Mount Edgecombe in Devon, for example, a visitor noted that the park was so extensive that 'it will require four hours' to visit it, and that

if there are any ladies of the Party, on application to Lord or Lady Edgecombe, or in their absence to the Gardiner the night before, the Ladies may be accommodated with a one-horse-chaise.[8]

It is impossible to discuss in detail all the varied kinds of manuscript evidence available in archives. The best advice is the simplest: look at everything which might be relevant. Nor should printed sources, in libraries and local studies centres, be ignored. From the late eighteenth century, printed sale catalogues began to appear, and these often tell us a good deal about the landscape around a country house; although of course, like the descriptions of properties supplied by modern estate agents, these have to be taken with a substantial pinch of salt. The county histories of the eighteenth and nineteenth centuries – which describe the ecclesiastical and manorial history, and principal antiquities, of each parish – only rarely allude to gardens. Often, however, they describe the changing ownership of estates and provide details about the constructional history of a country house. Both can be important in understanding the development of a landscape, because changes in the architecture of the house or in its ownership, often coincided with significant alterations to the gardens. Indeed, all the background information which these and the other sources discussed above can supply is important in order to see the development of a garden in its context – to see how its expansion, for example, was related to the changing fortunes of its owners, or to changing patterns of landownership in a parish.

Fieldwork: archaeology

A good deal can be learnt about the history of a park or garden from documents, maps and illustrations, but this information is always incomplete. Some things were never written down, many documents were thrown away by later generations and, as we have seen, it is often unclear whether plans and illustrations show something that actually existed, or represent unexecuted proposals. For all these reasons archive research always needs to be combined with an investigation of the landscape itself, and this is a task which is full of excitement and interest – and surprises.

Landscape parks consisted, and often still largely consist, of areas of grass and woodland. They are, therefore, good places to look for earthworks – that is, the humps and bumps caused by various past human activities, such as the ploughing or hedging of fields, the construction of houses or the extraction of mineral deposits. Earthworks only survive in areas which have, since the activity which created them, been left undisturbed by later ploughing or building.[9]

Many earthworks found in parkland were created long before the park itself came into existence. Occasionally such remains are of great antiquity, for instance Rushmore park (Dorset) contains a number of prehistoric features, including Bronze Age barrows, a Bronze Age enclosure, field systems and boundaries.[10] But such discoveries are rare. Most surviving parks were created around houses that lay in areas which had been farmed intensively for centuries, and the earthworks they contain relate to the medieval or post-medieval landscape. Deserted settlements are quite a common discovery. Such sites consist of complexes of low banks defining the principal property boundaries, wide 'hollow ways' marking the main roads and tracks, and – sometimes – low mounds indicating the sites of the houses themselves. Some earthworks of this kind represent settlements cleared away to make way for the park; others, however, mark places abandoned long before.

Much more common are the traces of early fields and roadways. In regions where the arable fields were ploughed in ridges, most notably the Midlands, areas of 'ridge and furrow' are often visible. Good examples can be seen in Wimpole park (Cambridgeshire) (Fig. 4). Not all open-field strips were ridged, but even when they

4 *Wimpole Park (Cambridgeshire): 'ridge and furrow' earthworks, the former ploughlands of the village open fields, preserved under the parkland turf.*

were not soil usually built up at the junctions between the furlongs, as ploughs were cleaned and soil was shaken from the hooves of the draught animals. This led to the build-up of long, low banks, usually referred to as 'heads' or 'headlands', and these too are often encountered. Most parks were not, however, created at the expense of open fields. Many areas of England were never farmed in this way, and even where they had been, this form of agriculture had usually disappeared long before the park was made. Most surviving parks originated in the period after 1740, by which time the kinds of parishes in which they were being created – those dominated by a rich, resident landowner – had already been enclosed, that is, divided into fields by walls or hedges. Estate accounts often record payments made for 'levelling the banks and filling the ditches' when parks were laid out, but some

archaeological trace usually remains, in the form of scarps or banks, or slight linear depressions. These, like all earthworks, are most clearly visible in the winter, when the grass is short, and when the sun is low in the sky. Holloways marking former roadways are usually more easy to spot, for they were much harder to obliterate, being more massive features. Many other earthworks can be discovered in the parkland turf, including the mounds of windmills, and pits and ponds with a wide variety of origins.

All parkland earthworks are interesting and important in their own right, especially in the mainly arable areas of eastern England, for here parks are often the only extensive areas of grassland, forming islands of archaeological interest in the otherwise unrelieved arable. Moreover, where early maps are absent, such archaeological evidence may provide the only clue to the layout and development of the pre-park landscape. An examination of such earthworks should not be neglected even by those whose only interest is the history of garden design. For the earlier landscape had an important, often decisive, effect on the design of the park itself. The hedgerow now marked only by the low bank once contained trees, and these were usually incorporated within the new landscape, their position influencing the artistic decisions of the designer. And the disposition of clumps of planting might, on occasions, be determined less by abstract aesthetic considerations than by the need to hide earlier marl or gravel pits.

Some of the most interesting earthworks found in parks relate to earlier phases of gardening activity on the site. These come in a variety of forms, depending on the size, date and style of the garden in question.[11] The larger geometric gardens of the sixteenth and seventeenth centuries involved a great deal of earth movement in order to make terraces, raised walkways and 'mounts', or circular viewing platforms. Great gardens of the early eighteenth century also made extensive use of terraces, but in addition had sunken fences, or 'ha-ha's', and large geometric water features. Their creation, moreover, was often accompanied by quite massive alterations to the natural landforms at some distance from the garden itself in order to open up vistas or allow for the passage of avenues. Garden earthworks do not only occur in parks. They can also be found in places where elite residences declined in importance, or disappeared altogether, during the seventeenth and eighteenth centuries (Fig. 5). Indeed, the best preserved of these earthworks are usually found in such locations. Where country houses have continued to be occupied, the traces of early gardens were often badly damaged, or entirely destroyed, when the 'natural'

5   *Strixton (Northamptonshire): the terraces of a seventeenth-century garden laid out around Strixton Manor (now demolished).*

landscape park became fashionable in the later eighteenth century.

It is in such places, too, that walls and garden buildings from the period before 1750 are most likely to have escaped demolition. Many houses which were important in the sixteenth and seventeenth centuries later declined in status and the walled garden courts survived as farmyard enclosures. On more successful sites these would have been swept away. Careful investigation of such structures can reveal a great deal about the development of early gardens which is less obvious, or absent altogether, in the documentary sources. Indeed, the same can be true of the 'hard

landscaping' of the nineteenth-century garden: terraces, balustrading and paths often repay careful examination, for they too can have a more complex history than at first meets the eye.

The examination of earthworks, and of 'standing structures' like walls and garden buildings, is not the only archaeological method which can throw light on the history of gardens. Aerial photographs – held by the County Archaeological Units or at the Cambridge University Aerial Photograph Library for instance – can also be very informative. They show not only earthworks but also the parch-marks, produced in particularly dry summers, of

6   *Raynham (Norfolk): outlines of the seventeenth-century garden revealed as parch-marks to the east (left) of the hall.*

long-vanished walls, paths, garden buildings and even flower beds (Fig. 6). Excavation, too, is beginning to produce important information, especially about gardens of the sixteenth and seventeenth centuries, as at Kirby Hall (Northamptonshire), Castle Bromwich (Birmingham) and Temple Cressing (Essex), but also about those of the last century, as at Audley End (Essex). This approach is not, however, suitable for those untrained in excavational techniques, or who lack the resources for analysing, processing and storing the material (and especially any preserved botanical material) recovered.

Fieldwork: plants

Trees and plants form the most important part of any designed landscape but they are also the most ephemeral. They either die or are replaced as fashions change. Indeed, planting schemes are inherently unstable, and have to be constantly managed. The more 'unnatural' the design, the sooner neglect becomes evident. The highly formal gardens of the seventeenth century, with their clipped shrubs, box-edged geometric flower beds and pleached trees, would have betrayed the absence of the gardener's hand within a month, whereas landscape parks could survive for centuries with little more than regular grazing, timber management and occasional dredging of the lake. Yet even these simpler landscapes change constantly. Their vistas and panoramas are continuously modified, not by the hand of the designer, but by the natural cycles of the plants themselves.

Indeed, what can be seen in the landscape today is usually very different from what the original designer saw, or planned. Even comparatively recent planting schemes have often changed out of all recognition. Areas of ornamental woodland or shrubbery created in the late nineteenth century are one

example – these are now rather unpopular features, solid, dull and gloomy, characterized by various kinds of evergreen. But to a large extent this is the consequence of later changes. The flowers which once bordered the walks running through them have long given way to invasive ivy and briars. The more tender flowering shrubs, which required light, have been progressively overshadowed by the growing canopy of cedar and pine, and have also disappeared. There are usually still remnants of the more hardy shrubs, particularly rhododendron and snowberry, and others able to tolerate reduced light values. But conifers of various sorts, as well as box, yew and laurel, are now the dominant elements in such designs, together with more recent arrivals, invasive elder and sycamore.

The herbaceous plants found in parks and gardens are invariably of comparatively recent origin, planted in the twentieth or, rarely, the late nineteenth century. When investigating the history of a designed landscape the main focus of attention is therefore the trees. An examination of these can tell us an enormous amount about the development of the landscape.

The land on which a new park or garden was laid out would almost always have contained some trees already. These were planted for practical reasons: to produce wood and timber, to provide shelter or mark boundaries. But they were often incorporated as aesthetic features within the new, designed, landscape, and examples of such ancient timber – usually oaks, sometimes ash or beech – can often be found within parks. They are identifiable by their great age and often by the fact that they were originally pollarded, that is, repeatedly cut back to the stem or bole at a height of around 1.5 or 2m (5 or 6ft), in order to produce a regular crop of poles, straight, thin-sectioned wood, suitable for burning, fencing, and a host of other everyday uses.

7 *Old pollarded oaks in Windsor Park.*

Although pollarding would usually have ceased when the tree was incorporated within the park, the resultant pattern of growth, with the branches springing from a callus (or bulbous damaged area) is usually clearly apparent (Fig. 7). Because such trees often stood in hedgerows, they now stand in rough lines, and often on the low ridges or banks which, as already described, mark the positions of hedges which were removed when the park was created.

Although ancient survivors like these can be found in many parks, most trees were planted as part of a design. This, however, does not mean that they were entirely ornamental in purpose. As well as being objects of beauty, many were also valued as commercial timber. Careful inspection of

clumps and belts will often reveal that the trees within them are mostly younger than those on the margins; the latter were not felled so willingly because of their importance in the view. And in general terms, trees within belts and plantations are – for the same reason – usually younger than those standing in the open parkland.

Woods and belts usually contained a range of native hardwoods such as oak, ash and beech, together with some softwoods. In contrast, trees planted in the more visible areas had less commercial importance and a much wider range of ornamental trees can be found in avenues, arboreta (tree collections) and pleasure grounds immediately around the house. The trees used for such features were much more susceptible to changes in fashion than those planted in the more distant areas of parkland and the species used in them can to some extent indicate the period the features were established, at least in their present form. For instance, an exotic ornamental cannot have been planted in a pleasure ground before it was introduced into this country.

The identification of some of these trees can pose considerable headaches, even for those with long experience and equipped with the right handbook.[12] This is particularly true of trees planted in the period after 1850. In some arboreta, such as Nuneham Courtenay (Oxfordshire) and Westonbirt (Gloucestershire), the trees carry labels giving their species and sometimes even the date when they were planted. Would that all pleasure grounds and arboreta were so blessed. In practice, a small, but nevertheless annoying, minority of exotics prove impossible to identify with complete confidence.

Fashions in tree-planting changed in complex ways through the centuries. Sweet chestnut and lime were very favoured as ornamental trees in the seventeenth and early eighteenth centuries, but rapidly fell out of favour, probably because they were associated with the features – avenues and wildernesses – which, as we shall see, became unfashionable as the eighteenth century progressed. Some species considered ornamental by one generation were shunned, or considered simply utilitarian, by the next. Sycamore, for example, was highly prized in the sixteenth and seventeenth centuries (Fig. 8) but has progressively declined in status to the point where it is now considered as little more than a weed.

Parkland trees have their own 'archaeology'. Their present form provides clues about the way they were managed in the past. It was rare for parkland trees to be pollarded, as this form of management was, by the eighteenth century, associated in

8　*Newburgh Priory (Yorkshire): one of the ancient sycamores in the gardens to the north of the house. This probably stood on the edge of a seventeenth-century 'grove', or ornamental wood. The unusual growth pattern suggests that it once formed part of a hedge.*

the minds of owners with the working agricultural landscape – precisely the kind of appearance the owners of parks were trying to avoid. Most trees were allowed to grow as standards, with long straight unbranched trunks, a practice which also provided the maximum amount of good commercial timber. But some were managed to produce other aesthetic effects. One common practice was 'heading', a horticultural technique used from at least the early eighteenth century. Cutting back of the leading shoot and judicious pruning of side branches when the tree was young resulted in a mature tree with a widely spread head but (unlike pollards) with a consistent size of bole and branch. Oak, elm, sweet chestnut and lime appear to have been the species most commonly treated in this way, although there are also considerable numbers of headed beech. This latter tree is, however, prone to rot in the branch nodes and heading has, over time, often proved very destructive (Fig. 9). The practice was also employed in avenues, partly because it ensured an even height to the trees.

Headed trees, sometimes referred to by confused surveyors as 'Giraffe Pollards' (they were usually cut at a height of 2.5–3m (8–10ft), way above the reach of the average wood-gatherer) are sometimes difficult to distinguish from those resulting from another technique used to produce trees with a wide crown: the planting of two (or occasionally more) young trees in the same hole. This was widely practised in the late eighteenth and nineteenth centuries, to give

trees growing in the open parkland an irregular, romantic, picturesque appearance. Careful inspection will usually reveal the lines where the trunks have fused, particularly in the case of beech, which responds exceptionally well to this treatment.

The older trees in a park, especially those growing in the vicinity of the house, sometimes show signs of more drastic forms of past management. Before the middle decades of the eighteenth century, trees and shrubs in gardens were frequently topiaried – that is clipped into unnatural, geometric forms – or used to create various kinds of hedge, or a hedge-like feature. Any plant which has been shaped or regularly cut in these ways bears the marks of this practice until it is felled or loses its branches. Trees, especially limes, growing beside walks and

9 *An avenue of 'headed' beeches: typically, the second tree is suffering extensive damage and has a split bole.*

10 *Chiswick House, London: a nineteenth-century pleached lime walk.*

in avenues were frequently pleached: that is, pruned in one plane to form a kind of aerial hedge. Such trees have larger limbs in one direction than in another, and show signs of callus development similar to that on a pollarded tree (Fig. 10). Trees originally forming a hedge – especially beech, hornbeam and yew – display a similar damaged layer, but low down, usually 1m (3ft) or so above the ground, and similar uneven growth in different planes. It is also possible to identify trees which were formerly managed as topiary, most commonly yews, as many of those planted in the last century have multiple branches growing at a low level. The signs become more blurred with age, but the 'marks of the scissors' are not easily erased.

The form of a tree does not only provide information about how it was managed in the past, but also about the way in which its immediate environment has changed over the years. A tree growing in woodland is characterized by a tall, unbranched trunk. If the woodland is later removed from around it, any additional side growth will be significantly smaller than the crown, and the overall effect will still be broadly columnar. In contrast, free-standing parkland trees tend to put on side branches at a lower level than those in woods. If they later become embedded in woodland, they usually maintain this branched appearance, and stand out clearly from their bare-stemmed neighbours. This kind of information can be particularly important when attempting to estimate the age of trees.

The only certain way of finding out the age of a tree is to count the annual growth rings in a section of trunk, although even this can be unreliable in the case of certain trees, most notably lime, which in some years add rings so small that they can only be detected through microscopic examination. But to see the rings at all, either the tree has to be cut down, or a core taken through its trunk. The latter method can cause damage to the tree, is time-consuming and requires special equipment; the former is simpler, but more drastic! A much more convenient and practical, but unfortunately less accurate method, is 'girthing'. If the circumference of a tree is measured at chest height, its age can be estimated using the formula developed by Alan Mitchell.[13] Broadly speaking, a free-standing parkland tree will have 2.5cm (1in) of girth for every year of its age. Woodland timber, however, puts on girth at a rather slower rate, and for trees in belts and plantations two years of age for every 2.5cm (1in) of girth has to be allowed. The growth of trees in avenues, or in small clumps, falls in between these two extremes. But the problem is that the pattern of planting within a park can change over time, so that a tree which once stood in open parkland might come to be surrounded by woodland; or, conversely, woodland can be thinned so that some of the constituent trees become parkland standards. Such changes can often be picked up from maps and documents, but examination of the tree's growth pattern, in the ways discussed above, can also prove helpful.

Even when such allowances are made the method is not very reliable, even as a rough rule of thumb. If a tree is growing on particularly fertile soils, or on a sheltered south-facing slope, it will put on girth at a faster rate than the rule predicts. Conversely, a tree maturing in an environment with a poor water supply, or choked with undergrowth, will grow less quickly. Pruning and pollarding reduce the lateral growth rate, and massive pollards are actually older than they look – here, again, is a demonstration of the importance of looking at the growth pattern of the tree in estimating its age. Different species, moreover, respond differently to factors of local climate or topography: what might admirably suit hornbeam may impede the growth of beech, for example. Some species do not conform to a rule; the most extreme case is the yew, individual specimens of which display considerable and apparently random variations in the rate at which they increase in girth. And, last but not least, the method does not seem to work at all well with conifers, especially those introduced from abroad.

The method can, however, provide much useful information if used with care. Within any park, trees of the same species, growing in similar locations, will tend to increase their girth at roughly the same rate. If some of these can be dated by other means – through maps, accounts, documents, or by counting the rings of felled specimens – then the age of otherwise undated trees can be estimated with some confidence. As with the other kinds of evidence discussed in this chapter, girth-dating of trees proves most valuable when combined with information from all other sources: it is one more piece of the jigsaw.

Girth measurement can thus help to isolate broad phases of planting activity across a landscape. It can also be useful in helping to understand the history of an individual feature, like an avenue, especially if felled specimens are also available to provide a ring count. Trees in avenues die, or are brought down by gales, and need to be replaced. Some avenues were extended some time after their original planting. The lime avenue in Cassiobury Park, Watford (Hertfordshire) is often thought to be that planted by Moses Cook, and mentioned in his book of 1676 (Fig. 11).[13] Micro-analysis of the rings on some of the largest trees show that they could not have been planted before 1713.[14] Girth-measurements clearly reveal two main subsequent phases of

11 *Cassiobury, Watford (Hertfordshire): this lime avenue, reputedly planted by Moses Cook in the 1670s, was probably established early in the following century.*

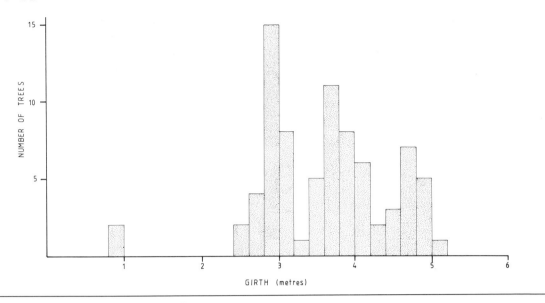

12 *Cassiobury, Watford (Hertfordshire): a graph showing the girths of the surviving trees in the lime avenue. The graph shows clear clusters of girths, suggesting that the avenue was extensively replanted on two occasions, probably around 1760 and again in the early decades of the nineteenth century.*

replanting, probably in the 1760s or 1770s, and again around 1820 (Fig. 12).

Few avenues, clumps or belts contain precisely the same trees that they were originally planted with. Most park woodlands initially contained large numbers of conifer 'nurses' which were thinned and removed long ago. Elms have vanished from clumps and woods as well as from open parkland. Features in a design can be very long-lived but individual trees within them are much more susceptible to change.

Fitting it all together

The history of a park or garden only really begins to emerge as all these different sources of information – cartographic, documentary, archaeological and botanical – are brought together. This is the most enjoyable part of the whole exercise and one of the best methods is to draw up a series of maps, all to the same scale. For a large site, 6 inch to the mile (or 1:10,000) is usually sufficient, for smaller or more complex landscapes, 25 inch (or 1:2500) is better. One map will show the archaeological features discovered, another the various girths of trees recorded. Estate, tithe and other early maps can then be redrawn to the same scale, and by comparing one map with another, it is possible to relate the different sources of evidence, testing and amplifying each in turn. Thus, for example, an earthwork discovered in a park might be found to occupy the same site as a long-demolished garden building shown on an early map, thereby both interpreting the earthwork and confirming that the building in question was actually constructed, rather than merely a proposal. The documentary evidence can then be brought in to play, to illuminate or modify the picture presented by the other sources. At the end of all this work, two overriding impressions usually remain: the history of any designed landscape is incredibly complex, and no garden remained the same for any length of time.

2 Early gardens in England

Medieval gardens

Archaeological evidence from Fishbourne (Hampshire), Frocester (Gloucestershire) and elsewhere shows that ornamental gardens existed in England during the Roman period. Anglo-Saxon kings and magnates also may have had them, but it is only after the Norman Conquest that we first learn about them from documents. In or around the year 1092, William Rufus and his courtiers visited Romsey Abbey 'to look at the roses and the flowering herbs', and numerous later documents refer to the gardens associated with palaces, castles, manor houses and monasteries.[1] These gardens came in a variety of forms, and unless described in detail the precise nature of an area called a *hortus* or a *herbarium* is often unclear. Some were purely functional, producing food or (especially in monasteries) medicinal herbs. Some, on the other hand, were entirely ornamental. But many were mixed, like that described by the thirteenth-century physician Henricus Anglicus. This *herbarium* was square, with borders running round each side, in which no less than 94 varieties of flowers, aromatics, salads, pot-herbs and medicinal herbs were cultivated together. Thus the third border contained plants as diverse as hollyhock, marshmallow, purple flag, horseradish, dill, wild thyme, mint, and houseleek.[2]

Medieval gardens, whatever their contents, were usually small, enclosed spaces. They often occupied the spaces and courtyards left between the buildings in a castle or palace. Where they did not, they were frequently surrounded on all sides by walls, fences or hedges. The plants within them grew in square or rectangular beds or borders, and many gardens contained raised benches of turf, sown with such low-growing flowers as trefoil, camomile and daisy. The beds were often arranged round a square lawn, with a central fountain or sundial. Trellis work, arbours and gravel paths were also important features.[3] Such gardens were structured spaces, intended to stimulate all the senses, but quite cut off from the everyday world around them.

Royal gardens are – as might be expected – the best documented. Thus at Windsor Castle, accounts provide numerous references to gardening activity, starting in 1156, when 11s was paid for 'the work in the vineyard and garden'. By 1206, under Henry III, £30 was being spent on 'the King's garden', and glass windows were being inserted into Queen Eleanor's chamber 'facing on to the King's herb garden'. By this time, there was a cloistered garden, and a 'herbarium' in the lower bailey, both turfed, and from 1237 there was a salaried gardener. The turf was constantly being maintained or replaced: thus in 1320 Adam the gardener dug up 3300 turfs to lay in the cloister garden, and also repaired the gate leading into it and the wooden palings that enclosed it. There was another garden, enclosed by hedges and paling, beyond the castle ditch, which was reached by a bridge. In 1246 two gardeners were paid 2½d a day (a good wage) for making a 'fair shrubbery' there, although much of the area was used as a vineyard.[4] Thus by the middle of the thirteenth century Windsor had a range of gardens, and the same was true of other royal and also baronial residences. There is a fair amount of evidence to suggest that medieval gardens were particularly associated with women, and that queens and great ladies took an active role in their design and management. For example, Eleanor of Castille, the wife of Edward I, brought gardeners trained in Moorish traditions of courtyard and fountain gardening to the royal palace of Kings Langley (Hertfordshire). In 1280 she was importing grafts of apple trees from Aquitaine, and making a new vineyard garden, complete with a gardener's house.[5]

There were some larger, more open designs for medieval gardens, often referred to as 'pleasances'. The large new garden created by the Abbot of Peterborough in 1302 contained a wide range of flowering plants, and was surrounded by two concentric moats, the space between them planted with pear trees.[6] The ornamental grounds around Lanthony Priory, just outside Gloucester, extended for nearly a kilometre: 'a place so beautiful and peaceful, provided with fine buildings, fruitful vines, set about handsomely with pleasure gardens and orchards'.[7]

This kind of documentary information only exists for the residences of the royal and baronial elite, and for some monastic institutions. Minor manor houses certainly had gardens – they are often referred to in documents – but their appearance, and in particular the relative balance of aesthetic and functional features within them, is unclear. Only a few manorial gardens have left clear earthwork traces. One example is at Collyweston (Cambridgeshire), where low terraces around the site of the manor house probably relate to gardens laid out in 1453–4, although remodelled to some extent in 1486.[8] It is possible, however, that above-ground traces of manorial gardens are more common in the landscape than we realize.

Christopher Taylor has suggested that some medieval moats – the familiar rectangular or sub-rectangular ditched enclosures frequently encountered in the countryside – may represent gardens.[9] Most surrounded important houses, the homes of manorial lords or prosperous yeoman farmers; but some, when excavated, reveal no evidence of occupation, and may have surrounded gardens associated with neighbouring houses which were enclosed in other ways. In some places, two adjacent, or conjoined, moats are found, as at Linwood (Lincolnshire). In such cases, one perhaps surrounded the house, the other the garden. Certainly, both contemporary documents and continental illustrations suggest that some gardens were moated. Moats would have helped drain a garden located on damp or heavy soils, as well as affording a measure of protection from the depradations of wild or domestic animals.

Virtually nothing is known about the gardens of the medieval peasantry. Such evidence as there is suggests that they were mainly used for the cultivation of vegetables (principally of the cabbage and onion families) and herbs, although they may well have contained some aesthetic features.[10] The 'crofts' – the rectangular earthwork enclosures which can be seen behind the house sites in deserted medieval villages – must in part have been used as gardens, although some were also paddocks, or even ploughed as arable land. Occasionally, however, their horticultural function seems clear: at the deserted site of Hound Tor on Dartmoor, the enclosures adjoining the house sites had entrances so narrow (0.3m

(1ft) or less in width) that animals would not have been able to enter them.[11]

Deer parks

Medieval deer parks have left much clearer traces in the modern landscape than gardens. Parks were, essentially, hunting-grounds and venison farms, enclosed with a substantial earthwork bank and ditch, which was surmounted by a fence of cleft oak stakes, a hedge or a freestone wall. Such barriers were usually substantial. They had to be, for deer can leap 3m (10ft) vertically, or 6m (20ft) horizontally. Parks were mainly located on the more agriculturally marginal land in any area, and consisted of rough open pasture, wood-pasture and enclosed woodland. Most were created out of waste land, although in the more populous areas of the country, especially East Anglia, they were sometimes carved out of part of the lord's arable land. Most, but not all, were located at some distance from their owner's residence, and they generally contained a 'lodge'. This was a complex of buildings providing accommodation for hunting parties as well as for the keeper who maintained the park and its stock, and kept out poachers.[12] Not all of the latter were starving peasants. Hunting in another man's park was the supreme affront, and a well-established method of showing disrespect for rival members of the gentry or aristocracy. For parks were symbolic landscapes, expressions of power and prestige, and the lodge itself was thus normally moated, demonstrating its importance and its status as an elite building.

Most parks covered an area of between 30 and 80ha (75 and 200 acres), although some were considerably larger. Clarendon (Wiltshire) for example, had a circumference of over 13km (8 miles). Some, conversely, were considerably smaller, and examples covering as little as 5 or 10ha (12 or 25 acres) were by no means unknown. In parks as small as this, hunting would not have been possible. Indeed, even a park of 20ha (50 acres) would not have provided much in the way of an exhilarating chase. The smaller parks must have been used to keep deer prior to being hunted across the adjacent farmland, or else served simply as venison farms.

Parks were complex landscapes, with many functions. In addition to deer they often contained some sheep or cattle; they produced timber and wood; and many contained fishponds. Parks were essentially a Norman creation, although late Saxon England had known enclosures, *hagas*, for coralling deer prior to hunting, and perhaps for their protection during breeding.[13] By the time of Domesday, there were at least 35 parks in England. Their numbers grew thereafter, particularly during the boom years of the thirteenth century, and by 1300 there may have been as many as 3000 in the country, although they were not evenly distributed. They were thick on the ground in the West Midlands, and in the south-east of England and the Home Counties. There were fewer in the Midland, 'champion' areas of England, dominated by arable farming in 'regular' open fields. They were also noticeably rare in areas characterized by a high density of free tenures, and by complex patterns of manorial organization, most notably Lincolnshire, East Anglia and Cambridgeshire. There were also relatively few in remote areas of the north and west, such as Northumberland, Cumberland, Durham, Devon and Cornwall.[14]

Some medieval parks developed into landscape parks. Most were 'disparked', converted to agricultural use, in the late- or post-medieval period. Why deer parks declined in number at this time is not entirely clear. It may have been for economic reasons – as population levels fell, wages, and therefore maintenance costs, rose. The climatic deterioration which occurred at this time may have had an effect on the fallow deer, the main occupants of the parks, by encouraging certain kinds of parasite. Whatever the precise reason, most medieval parks disappeared, although they have often left their mark on the modern landscape. Occasionally their walls survive, as at Beckley (Oxfordshire), Moulton (Northamptonshire) or Newton Blossomville (Buckinghamshire).[15] More often, the boundary bank survives as an impressive earthwork, or as a hedge-bank larger and more sinuous than those surrounding the adjacent fields.

Sometimes this bank still clearly defines the characteristic oval or sub-rectangular outline of the park, although this shape – probably intended to cut down on fencing costs and to prevent the deer from being hemmed into a corner too early in a hunt – was never quite as ubiquitous as some books on landscape history suggest. The roughly oval outline was generally a feature of parks which had been laid out in extensive tracts of open waste. Where parks were created in a more cluttered and subdivided landscape, in the more densely-settled areas of England, their shape was affected by adjacent fields and holdings and they had a more indented and thus less obvious outline. But even in these cases, the former presence of a park is often given away by certain characteristic field-names: park field, park gate field, lodge close, or lawn (from *launde*, the term for an area of open pasture within a park).

From the discussion above, it might seem that medieval deer parks were very different from later landscape parks; that they were economic and recreational, rather than aesthetic, landscapes, and that they were quite distinct from contemporary gardens. Recent research, however, suggests a more complex and subtle picture. Parks were the quintessential symbols of aristocracy. They expressed not only ownership of land, but ownership of land over which the rights of the wider community had usually been extinguished; a notable feature when most

of the country was occupied by commons and common fields. They were used for hunting large game, an activity long restricted to the elite. And they were expensive to maintain. As pre-eminent symbols of wealth and prestige, the distinctive, natural landscape of the park – areas of pasture, irregularly scattered trees, blocks of woodland – had an immense aesthetic appeal. Not surprising, then, that although most parks lay at a distance from the home of their owner, the greatest residences in medieval England – castles and royal palaces – were often set beside, or within, parks. At Woodstock (Oxfordshire) in 1354 a balcony was constructed specifically to give Princess Isabella an unrestricted view of the park.[16] Similarly, at Broughton (Oxfordshire) Bishop William of Wykeham built a belvedere in 1380, raised on two tall arches, so that he could look over the battlements at the game in 'The Warren' on the adjacent hillside.[17]

Moreover, from as early as the twelfth century, some royal parks contained important aesthetic features. Woodstock is a good example. The park was established by Henry I in 1110, and soon afterwards he created within it a menagerie containing lions, lynxes, leopards, camels and even a porcupine. Henry III replaced this with 'Rosamund's Bower', an elaborate maze-garden, which was subsequently developed into a cloistered water pleasance with moats and fountains. By the 1250s, this was connected to the palace by a long covered walkway. Here, as at other great palaces, the distinction between 'park' and 'garden' was clearly becoming blurred.[18]

The late Middle Ages

There are tantalizing hints that, in the late Middle Ages, the spread of gardens out into the wider surrounding landscape became more common. One example which still

13 *The Pleasaunce, Kenilworth (Warwickshire): the remains of the elaborate moated gardens constructed by Henry V in the early fifteenth century.*

survives in earthwork form is the detached pleasance constructed in 1414 by Henry V at Kenilworth (Warwickshire), 1km (½ mile) to the west of the castle. This covered an area of about 1ha (2½ acres), enclosed by a double moat, and contained a banqueting house and other buildings (Fig. 13). It could be reached from the castle by boat, for it stood at the end of the 'Great Mere', which is now drained but which was the largest of several interconnecting pools around the castle.[19] Conventionally considered to be part of the castle defences, these may well have been created during the fourteenth century as part of a scheme of aesthetic landscaping.

This certainly seems to have been the case at Bodiam Castle (Sussex). Here, a complex collection of earthworks and ponds appears to be the remains of elaborate water features constructed in the fifteenth century to enhance the appearance of the castle. Some 300m (1000ft) north of the castle site, on a ridge, a separate area of earthworks may mark the site of a pleasance which provided views of the castle, set within what has been described as a 'Spencerian fantasy landscape'.[20] Large ornamental areas of water around or beside other late medieval castles – such as Baconsthorpe (Norfolk) – may similarly represent the remains of large-scale aesthetic landscaping schemes. Such layouts, it must be stressed, were not common – they were usually only created around the homes of the very wealthiest in the land. Nor were they really 'gardens' in the normal sense of the word. But they do, nevertheless, show that medieval kings and great barons had the power and inclination to mould landforms on a scale comparable to Capability Brown and his contemporaries several centuries later.

There were other important developments in garden design during the late Middle Ages. From the 1470s the style of gardens – like that of buildings – was greatly influenced by fashions emanating from the court of the Dukes of Burgundy, who ruled Flanders and the Low Countries. Arbours became more important and more architecturally complex. Carved heraldic beasts, set on painted poles, became common. Topiary – shrubs cut to geometric shapes – began to appear. Above all, this period saw the appearance of 'knots' – geometric patterns defined by dwarf box, lavender or similar low-growing plants.

The last decades of the fifteenth century saw the appearance of viewing mounds, or 'mounts'. These provided an elevated prospect of the emerging geometric complexity of the garden. They were often placed in the corners of an enclosure, as in the garden laid out by one of the last Abbots of Glastonbury at Mells (Somerset) shortly after 1500.[21] This indicates that they were also often intended to provide views *out* of the garden, over the adjacent estate land and park. Several examples survive in England, although they are difficult to date. They continued to be constructed through the

seventeenth (e.g. Boscobel in Shropshire) and into the eighteenth centuries (as at Oakley Hall in Hampshire).

In short, elite gardens in the later Middle Ages were becoming both more complex and larger, although still for the most part small by later standards. Both these developments were encouraged by the establishment of the Tudor regime and with it the cessation of internal warfare. The gardens at Mettingham College, a monastic community in Suffolk, were probably fairly typical of those laid out around a moderately wealthy residence. A survey made in 1562, some twenty years after the college had been dissolved, recorded their decayed remains. The gardens were moated, and the largest, around 0.5ha (1¼ acres) in extent, was:

sett with diverse trees of fruite and devided into sondrye partes with quicksett hedges and quicke hedges of boxe where hathe byn manye fayer Arbors and many small gardens . . . and hathe fower little pondes in it called fridaye pondes [which] served to preserve fishe taken on [the] weken dayes tyll fridaye.[22]

Renaissance landscapes: 1550–1640

There is more information available about designed landscapes in the period after 1550. This is partly because of the proliferation of gardening texts and descriptions, and the appearance of plans and illustrations. But it is also because elite gardens continued to become larger and more complex, incorporating substantial terraces, mounts and water-gardens which have sometimes left clear archaeological traces. This is the case especially where the house with which they were associated disappeared, or declined drastically in status, before they could be systematically flattened to make way for later fashions in garden design.[23]

In some ways, gardens of this period continued the traditions of the medieval centuries. They were highly regular and geometric in layout, with straight gravel paths, knots, topiary and clipped hedges. But in other ways gardens, at least those created by the richest individuals, began to develop along new lines. Like houses, they were increasingly influenced by Renaissance ideas from Italy. Italian writers like Leon Battista Alberti considered that the garden should not simply be slotted into some convenient space around the house, but should be conceived as an integral part of its design, and should have an overall coherence and symmetry. In addition, Italian gardens were less inward-looking, and more varied in their structure, than those in late medieval England.

Italian villas were, where possible, built on rising ground, and their gardens made much use of terraces, providing wide views across the adjacent countryside. They also functioned as museums, displaying statues and architectural features plundered from the classical past, or the ruins of classical buildings adopted as garden features *in situ*. They frequently contained automata – complex and often amusing machines, powered by weights and water – and grottoes – artificial, cave-like structures. They were varied, sophisticated landscapes. Many gardens were laid out either side of a main axis, focused on the principal facade of the house. Near the house were the more rigidly designed areas, but with increasing distance, the layout became more irregular, with groves of woodland containing winding paths.[24]

Italian Renaissance ideas spread gradually through northern Europe, being altered and adopted by the ruling elites in each of the emerging nation states. England initially received ideas via France and Holland, adopting and modifying ideas which were already modifications of the Italian originals. But from the early years of the seventeenth century, increasing numbers of people experienced Italian landscapes directly, for the 'Grand Tour' was not entirely an

invention of the eighteenth century. When John Raymond, marvelling at the beauties and complexities of the Villa d'Este gardens in the 1640s, exclaimed 'This shall be my patterne for a Countrey seat', he was voicing the feelings of many early tourists.[25]

It was among the royal family and the court aristocracy that Renaissance ideas made their earliest and greatest impact. Indeed, throughout the sixteenth and seventeenth centuries the court seems to have set the trends in garden fashions. It is sometimes suggested that the process began with the great new gardens laid out by Henry VIII at Hampton Court between 1535 and 1538, but this elaborate collection of knot and herb gardens, with covered walkways and a massive mount (heaped over 250,000 bricks), was really only a more sophisticated version of gardens in the prevailing late-medieval mode. True Renaissance influence was felt only gradually, in the decades after 1550, and initially with the introduction of Italianate features into existing gardens. Thus at Kenilworth, in the 1570s, the existing garden was provided with terraces, fountains and obelisks, while at Theobalds (Hertfordshire), a few years later, the enclosed courtyard gardens were given a grotto, terraces and statuary.[26] But when, from 1580, Wollaton Hall (Nottinghamshire) was built for Sir Francis Willoughby, the gardens were designed from scratch, laid out around the new house with terraces and ballustraded stairways.[27]

Other great gardens of the 1580s and 1590s followed suit. Later developments have usually obliterated all traces of these, but several survive in the form of earthworks. Three such sites illustrate the principal characteristics of the greatest gardens of this period: those laid out by Sir Christopher Hatton around Holdenby Hall (Northamptonshire) between 1579 and 1587;[28] those made for Chipping Campden House (Gloucestershire) in the 1610s;[29] and

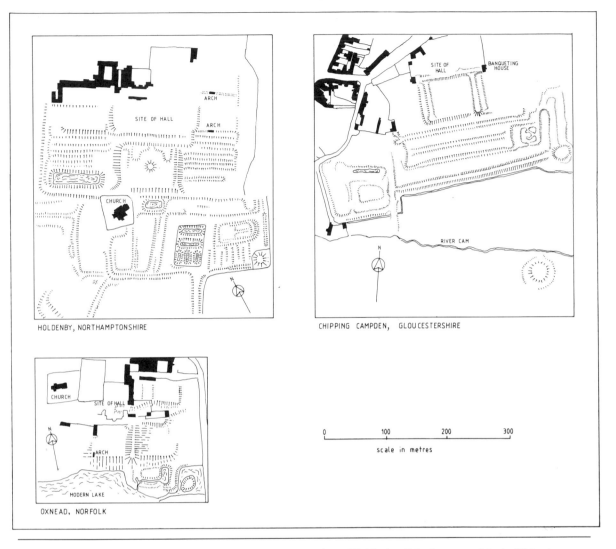

14 *The earthwork remains of three great Renaissance gardens: Holdenby (Northamptonshire), Chipping Campden (Gloucestershire), and Oxnead (Norfolk) (after RCHM and Paul Everson).*

those created by the Paston family beside Oxnead Hall (Norfolk)[30] in a number of stages from the 1590s into the 1630s (Fig. 14).

In all three cases, the great house stood on an eminence, overlooking a stream or river to the south. There were enclosed gardens to either side of the house, but a broad east-west terraced walk in front looked out over a wide, level, rectangular garden area, flanked by north-south terraces. There were other terraces – some of which were probably tree-lined walks – and water-gardens. The Renaissance inspiration of Oxnead and Holdenby was emphasized by the presence of imposing gateways, still surviving, which were loosely based on triumphal arches. All these gardens were, no doubt, replete with classically-inspired sculptures. At Oxnead the famous sculptor Nicholas Stone supplied a wide variety of statues in the 1620s, including representations of Hercules, Apollo, Juno and 'the 3 headed dogd Serbros with a petestall'. Like most great gardens of the period, those at Chipping Campden and Oxnead contained 'banquetting houses', for taking a banquet, an elaborate final course for a meal. Those at Oxnead have long since vanished, but those at Chipping Campden, placed at either end of the main terrace walk, still survive.

Not only did great terraced gardens like these provide extensive open views across the surrounding terrain; the local landscape was itself sometimes moulded aesthetically, to emphasize the grandeur of the house. At Holdenby, a section of the village which had been cleared to make way for the gardens

was rebuilt to a neat rectangular plan, and could be viewed through an arch from one of the garden enclosures. At Chipping Campden, the layout of roads within the adjacent town was extensively modified, to provide an imposing entrance to the new house.

Not all great gardens of the late sixteenth and early seventeenth centuries were like this. Imposing flights of terraces were more difficult to construct if the terrain was relatively level, and sometimes only a single terrace was possible. Moreover, as the seventeenth century progressed, some elite gardens began to emulate the axial structure of the Italian villa gardens. Isaac de Caus

15   *Wilton (Wiltshire): the garden designed by Isaac de Caus for the Earl of Pembroke in the 1630s.*

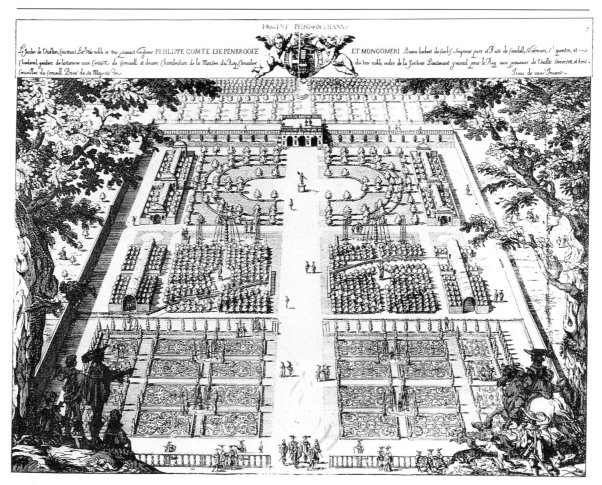

designed the gardens constructed in the early 1630s at Wilton (Wiltshire) for the Earl of Pembroke (Fig. 15).[31] The garden was an enclosed rectangle, divided into three sections. The first consisted of four 'Platts, embroidered', with flowers and statues. The second was a 'grove', densely planted with trees, containing statues and fountains. The third was laid out in formal walks, and ended in an imposing transverse terrace, beneath which was a grotto. What made this garden particularly 'Italianate' was the way in which it was laid out, symmetrically, either side of a broad walk, focused on the main facade of the house; and the way in which this walk was extended, beyond the terrace at the end of the garden, into an area of less regular groves and 'wildernesses', which contained an amphitheatre, a triumphal arch and a statue of Marcus Aurelius.

Another famous Italianate garden was that created by the Wentworth family in the 1610s and 1620s at Somerleyton (Suffolk). Although not very well known today (except for its important nineteenth-century gardens by W. A. Nesfield), this was described in Fuller's *Worthies of England* (published in 1662) as one of the three greatest gardens in the county. It is clearly illustrated on a fine estate map of 1652, and a schedule of 1663 provides some extra information.[32] The gardens were laid out on a single axis of symmetry at right angles to the main facade of the house, and became progressively more irregular in layout with increasing distance (Fig. 16).

The sequence began with the enclosed and geometric Great Garden. Next was the Orchard 'with the Terrace Walk at the south end thereof with the Banqueting Houses upon it', and beyond this a large square area planted with fir trees, called the 'Firrendale' or 'Fir Yard'. This was described in 1663 as being 'of late the most incomparable piece in the Realm of England, but now ruinated by a great wind'. It was planted in 1612 with 256 fir trees, probably in imitation of the evergreens used in Italian groves. Fuller was struck by this particular novelty, commenting that 'here *summer* is to be seen in the depths of *winter* in the pleasant walks, beset on both sides with fir trees green all the year long'. The large area north of the Fir Yard was described as 'the Wood and Walks with a variety of seats, statues, fish ponds, a house for pleasure newly erected and diverse other rarities'. This was a highly irregular 'wilderness' area, dissected with serpentine paths. There was also a grotto here.

In common with a number of other great houses of the period, Somerleyton had a detached pleasure ground, located over 1km (½ mile) to the south of the house. This was basically a water-garden, formed out of a 'broad' – a man-made lake which had been created centuries before by the flooding of medieval turbaries. There were a number of separate ponds, some with islands on which ornamental buildings were constructed. They were flanked by a terrace, along which ran a series of gravelled walks, while to the east was a mount. Much of this still survives in earthwork form. When first created, the garden must have been a fine place, a suitable setting for banquets or other *al fresco* entertainment.

Somerleyton Hall and its gardens were set within a deer park, a feature again shared with many elite residences. Parks were increasing in numbers again in the sixteenth and seventeenth centuries, but their role was changing. They were increasingly valued for their appearance. Deer were now being kept for their ornamental quality, and for venison, rather than for the pleasures of the chase, and cattle were becoming as numerous within them as deer. It was the sweeping natural irregularity of the park which was becoming its most valued feature, an appearance which contrasted sharply with the structure and symmetry of the gardens around the house.

There were further changes in the gardens

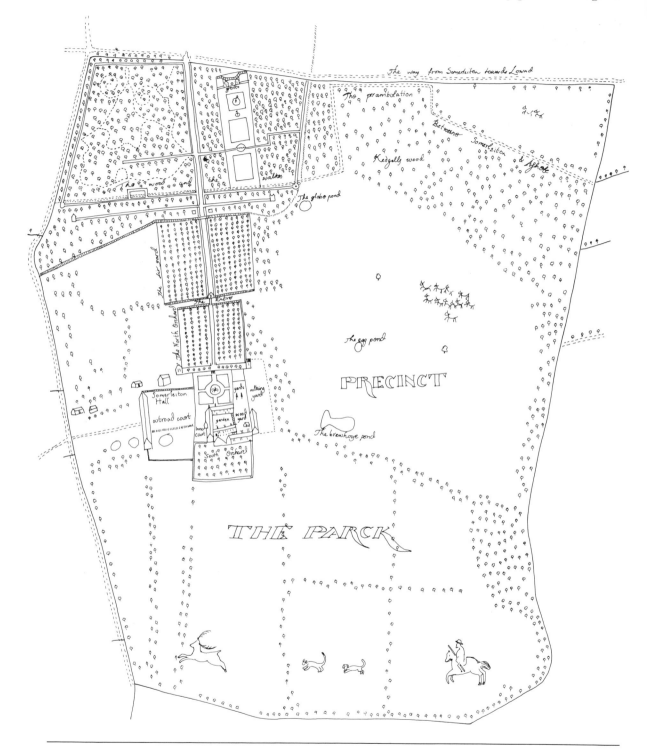

16 *Somerleyton (Suffolk): the great Italianate garden of the Wentworth family, as depicted on an estate map of*
1652.

themselves as the seventeenth century progressed. Documents describing the greatest gardens no longer refer to knots, but to 'parterres', designs in plants, turf and gravel which took three basic forms. *Parterres de broderie*, 'embroidered parterres', were the most elaborate and thus the rarest. These developed in France during the early decades of the seventeenth century. Like knots, they consisted of patterns defined by box or similar plants, with compartments filled with turf, coloured earth or flowers. But they formed more complex, flowing, arabesque designs, which were symmetrical around one axis rather than two. Usually, a number of separate units combined to form one design. *Parterres de piece coupe*, 'cutwork parterres', consisted of turf with patterns formed by beds for flowers. They were a particular feature of Dutch gardens. 'English parterres' – 'the meanest of all' according to one foreign commentator – were simply arrangements of turf and gravel.

Gardens like Wilton or Holdenby were expressions of political power, made by the greatest in the land. They were not typical of sixteenth- and early seventeenth-century gardens in England. Even among the richer landowners, 'Italianate' gardens, featuring imposing terraces, were not always favoured. This was sometimes because the nature of the local terrain made it difficult to construct them, but sometimes, apparently, out of conscious choice. Large gardens featuring such characteristic late-medieval features as corner mounts were still being laid out, as at Leighton Bromswold (Cambridgeshire), in the second decade of the seventeenth century.[33] The broad mass of the local gentry, moreover, had much more modest layouts. We have less information about these, but enough to know that they were usually hemmed in by high walls, fences or hedges; they did not make such extensive use of terraces with wide vistas over the surrounding countryside.

Remains of these more modest gardens

17 *Besthorpe Hall, Attleborough (Norfolk): one of three late sixteenth-century garden gates.*

can still be seen in many places in the form of enclosures surrounded by brick or stone walls. These walls are often quite elaborate, sometimes with decorative recesses and surmounted by decorative coping in the form of castellations or – in the case of those erected in the middle and later decades of the century – half-round bricks above simple dentilation. Considerable care and attention were lavished on gateways, and there are many surviving examples (Fig. 17). Garden buildings, such as small banqueting houses, might be placed against the sides, or in the corners, of an enclosure. A number, built of brick or stone, still stand (Fig. 18). Surviving gardens, and early maps, indicate

18 *Bawburgh (Norfolk): two late sixteenth-century garden buildings, formerly associated with Bawburgh Hall, now stand in the midst of a modern housing development.*

that walled enclosures often formed a chaotic, asymmetrical arrangement around a manor house, partly because they developed over time, with new courts being added in a somewhat piecemeal fashion by successive owners.

Documents and texts suggest that 'aesthetic' and 'horticultural' features were often thoroughly mixed in small manorial gardens of this period. Herbs and salads grew with flowers, while many minor gentlemen had 'wildernesses' which, consisting largely of fruit trees, were little different from orchards; or fishponds which also partly fulfilled the role of ornamental water-gardens.

Variations in garden design in this period were to some extent due to differences in wealth within the landed classes. But they also expressed important cultural differences: between the court aristocracy and their associates on the one hand, and the wider body of the local gentry on the other. The larger, more open, Renaissance designs of the former group expressed a confident dominance over the landscape surveyed from the Italianate terrace, and a knowledge of Renaissance civilization which marked them out from the mass of the population. The smaller, more enclosed gardens of the gentry, by contrast, represented their greater interest in horticulture – one aspect of a more general involvement in the details of domestic production and estate administration.

The differences in lifestyles, and values, between these two broad groups were one aspect of a wider and more complex range of social, political and religious divisions which, intensifying through the early seventeenth century, erupted in the 1640s in Revolution and republican dictatorship. Beginning as a dispute within the ruling classes, the struggle between Court and Parliament threatened, at times, to develop into a more wholesale social revolution, one which would have undermined the entire framework of property ownership and social inequalities on which, ultimately, the sophisticated grandeur of places like Holdenby or Somerleyton was based. Royal and royalist gardens were systematically vandalized by Parliamentarian troops, presumably because they symbolized the oppression and decadence of the Stuart regime. Massive fellings took place in parks confiscated by the revolutionary government. By the time of the Restoration in 1660, many great gardens and landscapes were in ruins. But then, in a climate of renewed stability, garden design entered a new phase of grandeur.

Garden design in the late seventeenth century

Evidence for garden design becomes abundant from the late seventeenth century. Large numbers of descriptions, plans and illustrations survive. Many garden walls, buildings and other structures, and even some of the original plantings, remain in the landscape. Restored to power, the royal court was once more the arbiter of fashion. Charles II had been exiled in France during the revolution, and was greatly influenced by the French interpretation of Italianate gardens, as developed by André Mollet, François Mansart, and André le Nôtre. William III, in contrast – who succeeded to the throne after a further constitutional crisis in 1688 – was a Dutch prince who came with ideas from his own country. Many books on garden history are thus eager to interpret late seventeenth-century English gardens in terms of 'French' or 'Dutch' influence.[34] But by the 1660s, these two 'national styles', in so far as they had ever been truly distinct, had become thoroughly mixed. And while foreign ideas were certainly important in this period, in many ways English gardens continued to develop along indigenous lines.

Indeed, the most significant development in this period was not so much the adoption of new ideas from abroad, as the overall increase in the scale of designed landscapes. Even in the Middle Ages, as discussed above, landforms were occasionally altered to enhance the appearance of a great castle. The landscape could also be manipulated on a large scale around the great houses and gardens of Elizabethan or Jacobean courtiers. But there was now an awareness, even among many of the local gentry, that the countryside around their demesnes could, and should, be treated aesthetically. In particular, avenues – which had been comparatively rare features in the landscape before 1640 – were now widely planted. Some still survive, although they have usually been extensively replanted. Most avenues are of lime (Cornbury (Oxfordshire), planted in 1664; Rougham (Norfolk), 1693); some are of sweet chestnut (Houghton (Norfolk), probably *c.*1700). Oak, elm, beech and ash were also planted, but less frequently. The trees were sometimes pleached, often headed. The greatest residences had several avenues, radiating out into the surrounding parkland.

When Crossley Park (Oxfordshire) was laid out between 1685 and 1688, seven avenues were planted, with another circling the park like a wheel, planted with alternate oaks and elms.[35] Lesser residences made do with fewer, which were planted across the adjacent fields. Often there was only one, although it could be of immense length. That at Rougham, composed of lime and ash, originally extended for nearly 1.8km (1 mile).[36] Focused on the main facade, such an avenue provided a striking frame in which to view the house, enhancing its grandeur when seen from a distance. But it also had a more complex symbolism, expressing the planter's ownership of all the land over which the avenue extended, and the fact that this land was enclosed; for it was almost impossible to establish trees in open fields or on commons, as the local inhabitants would simply remove them for firewood, or graze their livestock on them. Planting also expressed confidence in the security of possession, and in dynastic continuity, now that the arbitrary power of the crown had been curtailed and ideological discord reduced, if not entirely suppressed.

Indeed, avenues were only one facet of a more general upsurge in tree-planting. Following the advice of John Evelyn (and of the many subsequent writers who freely plagiarized his famous work *Silva*), landowners were increasingly occupied with the establishment of plantations in their parks and on their wider estate land. Woodland planted nearest the house was, of necessity, more ornamental in nature than

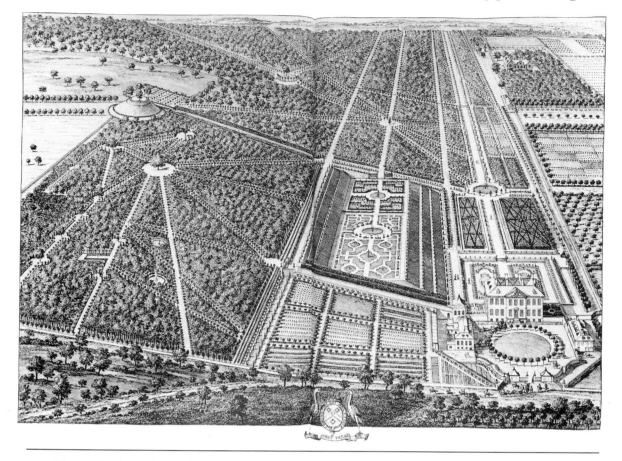

19 *New Park (Surrey): this illustration from Kip and Knyff's* Britannia Illustrata *gives a good impression of the appearance of large aristocratic gardens in England in the late seventeenth and early eighteenth centuries.*

that planted at a distance, and Kip and Knyff's *Britannia Illustrata* – a collection of engravings published in 1707, depicting some of the greatest seats in the land – reveals many examples of ornamental groves and wildernesses on the edge of the walled garden areas (Fig. 19).

All the illustrations in *Britannia Illustrata*, like most others made of country houses in this period, are bird's-eye views. This is an odd concept, on the face of it, given that no one ever saw these places from the air, but a necessary device to cope with the extensive and rigidly geometric quality of these landscapes. For not only did avenues and plantations spread over an ever-increasing

area; the walled enclosures themselves grew in size, and proliferated, creating complex collections of connected parterres. There had been large gardens before, but there were more of them now, and those around the greatest houses were very large indeed. Within or beside them, canals and geometric basins became common features. Often ascribed to Dutch influence, they owed at least as much to the fishponds and moats of English tradition, and were often created by adapting the latter. One of the best places to see canals from this period is Westbury Court (Gloucestershire).

Topiary – evergreen shrubs clipped into balls, obelisks and other geometric shapes –

was another standard feature at this time, and its popularity probably was in this case due to Dutch influence, although it had been a common enough feature of English gardens earlier in the century. The parterres were, for the most part, simple. *Parterres de broderie* were rare, and scarcely appear in contemporary illustrations. Cutwork parterres were more common, although often restricted to a single enclosure, a specialized garden for the cultivation and display of flowers. The dominant feature of most gardens was, in fact, the plain grass *plat*, bordered and dissected by gravel paths, which were often lined with topiary. A common arrangement, especially

20 *Ryston Hall (Norfolk): the gardens laid out around the hall built by Sir Roger Pratt in the early 1670s. From an undated painting of c.1680.*

CHESTER COLLEGE LIBRARY

21 *'The Falls', Harrington (Northamptonshire): the earthwork remains of a substantial garden, probably constructed in the 1680s.*

in smaller gardens, was to have a rectangular lawn divided into quarters by paths meeting at some central feature, like a fountain or a statue. Flowering shrubs and evergreens were planted in borders against the walls.

A number of contracts, drawn up when gardens were created or altered, survive from this period. They provide us with many details about the kinds of plants employed in these designs. At Raynham (Norfolk), around 1699, the new Parlour garden was to have

Quarters of Grass, and Borders Round ye Said Quarters in which Borders are to be planted a

Choice Collection of ye finest Sortes of Hardy Evergreens as is Undermentioned, with flowering Shrubs in the Borders next ye House: the 4 Borders next ye 4 Quarters of Grass, and ye other Borders in ye same Ground, to be planted with ye Varietye of Edgeings: the Grass and Gravell to be well laid to their most Proper levells, and ye Borders to be made with good Earth fitt to receive ye sevll plants.[37]

A note at the end of the document lists the 'Fine shaped hardy evergreens' (i.e. topiary) to be planted around the edges of the grass quarters: yews, 'strip'd' (that is, variegated) holly; juniper; 'cedar of Lycia'; laurel; and 'strip'd box'. The flowering shrubs for the border beside the house were to be 'Honeysuckles of sevll. Sortes', syringa (*Philadelphus coronarius*); 'cittisus secund clusy' (*Cytisus sessilifolius*); hypericum frutex (?*Hypericum hircinum*?); sweet briar; scorpion sena (*Coronilla emerus*); and althaea frutex (*Hibiscus syriacusus*). The paths were to be edged with 'Some of ye Sorts of Thymes; Thrift; Pincks; or Box'. At East Turnbull (Berkshire), in 1693, the borders in the various parts of the garden, and along the edges of the moat, were to be planted with firs, honeysuckle, cypress, Spanish broom (*Genista monosperma*), juniper, guelder rose, laburnum, lilac, hollies, sweet briar, phillyrea and jasmine. Here, again, there was to be a separate flower garden, surrounded by a holly hedge, containing a range of shrubs: laburnum, lilac, guelder rose, yellow jasmine, roses, barberry, 'gilded hollies', bay trees, mezerion (*Daphne mezereum*), honeysuckle, laurustinus (*Viburnum tinus*), yews, 'strip'd' box, and both 'strip'd' and 'plaine' phillyrea. There were also perennial flowers: buttercups, double anemones, jonquils (*Narcissus jonquila*), and 'other flowers to be worth at ye time when sett five pounds'.[38]

Yet in the gardens of the gentry, and to some extent in those of the greater landowners, the most prominent plants were not flowers, but fruit trees and bushes. These were present in prodigious numbers, and in many varieties. At East Turnbull, the orchard contained no less than 22 different varieties of apple, 12 of pear, 7 of cherry, 6 of plum, as well as quinces, medlars, mulberries, walnuts, currants, gooseberries and raspberries. In addition, the main garden areas included 40 other varieties of fruit trees, including numerous kinds of peach, nectarine and apricot. Over 450 individual trees were to be planted, plus 1100 fruit bushes. Such a diversity indicates something more than simple provision for household consumption. The collection and propagation of fruit trees was an important aspect of a gentleman's lifestyle.

Most gardens of this period were demolished as tastes changed in the following century. Walled courts, however, have survived in a number of places where houses have declined in status, and a number of fine avenues planted in this period still exist. There are earthwork traces too: one particularly fine example is the imposing series of terraces, locally known as 'the Falls', constructed around the manor of Harrington (Northamptonshire) in the 1680s (Fig. 21)[39]. As this example vividly shows, the gardens of the late seventeenth century could be vast, complex affairs. But the greatest flowering of the geometric tradition was yet to come.

3 The early eighteenth century

Gardens and society

Many books have been written about garden design in eighteenth-century England and, for the most part, the story they tell is a simple one.[1] A growing enthusiasm for 'natural' countryside, linked with an interest in creating landscapes like those portrayed in the paintings of Italian scenery by artists like Claude Lorrain, led to the progressive removal of geometric elements from the garden. Under the influence of successive writers and designers like Joseph Addison, Alexander Pope, Stephen Switzer, Charles Bridgeman and William Kent, straight lines gave way to serpentine ones, and walls were removed to open up views into the surrounding countryside. This process culminated in the decades after 1750 with the sweeping, irregular, 'natural' landscapes of 'Capability' Brown, in which the house stood free of walls and gardens, isolated in the park, marooned in an undulating sea of grass.

This traditional account is mainly based on the writings of contemporary intellectuals and designers, and on the descriptions and illustrations of a comparatively small number of famous and much-visited gardens. If we broaden our view and look at a wider range of landscapes and texts, a rather different picture emerges, at once more complex and more interesting. No single thread of fashion emerges; instead, a number of different styles of design were current during the early and middle decades of the eighteenth century.

In part, as in earlier centuries, this variety resulted from the different needs, lifestyles and wealth of different sections of the landed gentry. But it also seems to have been, in part, a reflection of the kind of political system which emerged in England during this period.

The political settlement of 1688, which brought William III to the throne, set the seal on the achievements of the Civil War. The king's power was limited in significant ways. He could not be a Catholic, he could not suspend the laws, he depended on Parliament for his finances and his ministers were answerable to Parliament. This settlement did not mean the end of disagreements within the landed classes. Factional struggles continued, although in more muted form. Contemporaries often described these in terms of a clash between 'Whigs' and 'Tories'. The former were characterized as supporters of the Protestant (and, after 1714, of the Hanoverian) succession; of a measure of religious toleration; and, after 1722, of a peaceful foreign policy. The Tories, in contrast, were supporters of the Stuart succession and, in some cases, of the supreme power of the Crown; and were widely suspected of crypto-Catholic sympathies. Such a simple description is a parody of a complex reality. Political rivalries within the landed elite were complex, and labels are rather misleading. Moreover, although there were real ideological issues at stake, much political activity was really about the clash between groups excluded from power, and those who controlled Parliament and had the ear of the king.[2]

Factional struggles were especially acrimonious under Queen Anne, but with the accession of George I in 1714, England entered upon a period of remarkable political stability. Under the astute leadership of the Whig Robert Walpole, England evolved through the 1720s and 1730s as a kind of one-party state. An increasingly complex state machine evolved, in which an expanding bureaucratic and military establishment was maintained by high levels of taxation. For many people the route to wealth lay through possession of a job, or a sinecure, in the government system. As these were firmly controlled by Walpole and his associates, they went to those with the correct political sympathies. This, coupled with astute management of Parliament, ensured a stable (if corrupt) climate in which the rich grew richer and more powerful: the larger landowners, merchants and financiers flourished.

Great landed estates became more consolidated, and grew in size at the expense of the smaller landowners. The latter were crippled by the burden of the land tax, instituted in 1692, and by the low agricultural prices caused by slow or stagnant population growth. It was among the marginalized lesser gentry – economically disadvantaged and perennially hostile to corrupt and centralizing administrations – that Tory magnates drew much of their political support.[3]

All this may seem rather irrelevant to the history of gardens. But it is not, for a number of reasons. Firstly, the new political circumstances meant that, to a large extent, the royal court lost its pre-eminent position as arbiter of gardening fashions. Secondly, even in the stable climate of the Whig hegemony, political intrigue continued, and

gardens, like great houses, were an important element in the political game. They could be used to express the dominance of the ruling group, and their fitness to rule. Equally they could be used by politically marginalized groups, as symbols of a moral challenge to the corruption of the political status quo.

As the estates of the great landowners grew in size, so too did their gardens and the growth in the scale of designed landscapes, already evident in the seventeenth century, continued apace. Aristocratic gardens needed to be large, to inspire awe among the local population and to impress the owner's 'interest', his political clients and supporters. Contemporary accounts reveal their success in achieving this. For it was a garden's magnificence, rather than its beauty or sophistication, which really impressed the visitor. Hamon le Strange positively drooled over the immensity of Wimpole (Cambridgeshire) in 1713:

Ye gardens are very fine and have cost a great summ of money having more walling for ye compass of ground than ever I saw.[4]

Significantly, visitors often attempted to estimate the scale of various features in a garden. One, at Blenheim, described:

the Gardens of 80 acres, ye middle gravel walk from ye House to ye End of ye Garden is 2220 feet long; ye many hedges in ye Gardens are said to be in Content near 20 measured miles . . .[5]

The late geometric garden

But as gardens grew larger, their style changed. Though still highly geometric, they became much simpler, less cluttered, and less enclosed, dominated by broad swathes of lawn, wide gravel paths, hedges and trees.

Groves or wildernesses were the most important feature in many of these gardens. Like those of the previous century, they

22 *Raynham (Norfolk): the wilderness, from an illustration of c.1725.*

were not the wild, irregular areas which their name might suggest, but small ornamental woods which were dissected by hedged gravelled paths, or *allées*. In the 1720s and 1730s they could often be found flanking the main axial vista to the house, often with their principal paths arranged in the form of a St Andrew's cross. Some time around 1725 Edmund Prideaux illustrated such an arrangement (rather badly) at Raynham in Norfolk – the home of Walpole's political ally and neighbour Horatio Townshend (Fig. 22). By chance, an undated contract describes the creation of this wilderness about 25 years earlier.[6] The neat clipped hedges on either side of the paths were originally planted with hornbeam, and the areas between – the 'Quarters' – were filled with 'several varieties of Flowering Tree' including limes, horse chestnut, wild service, guelder rose, lilac, bladder senna and wild olive, together with 'stript' (i.e. variegated) sycamore, and beech and birch. These were mixed with 'Silver Firs, Spruce Firs, Scotch Firs, Pine'.

Groves were endlessly varied: some were larger affairs, areas of commercial (and often pre-existing) woodland with paths and rides cut through them (Fig. 23). As the decades

passed they tended to become more complex in their layout, often including confusing, winding paths laid out according to what Batty Langley – whose book *New Principles of Gardening* summarized current practice in 1728 – called the 'artinatural line' (Fig. 24).[7]

Great gardens were now much more open to the outside world, more so even than great Italianate gardens of the sixteenth and seventeenth centuries like Holdenby or Oxnead. Walls were of limited importance: gardens were often bounded, in part, by a 'ha-ha'. This was seldom the discrete feature of the later eighteenth century, but a massive ditch, flanked by a terraced walk, often with projecting bastions modelled on those of contemporary fortifications. Walking around the perimeter of the garden, the owner or visitor would have enjoyed unrestricted views across the adjacent parkland. For parks continued to be a valued part of the aesthetic landscape around a great house. Indeed, their numbers seem to have been increasing once more in the decades after the Restoration, aided by the spread of enclosure and the increasingly consolidated nature of aristocratic estates.[8] The deer park continued to be an indispensable symbol of power and wealth, just as venison was a peculiarly aristocratic gift, sparingly doled out in return for political support. The savage Black Acts of the 1720s, which (among other things) made it illegal to buy and sell venison on the open market, served to further emphasize the aristocratic exclusivity of deer.[9] The increasing aesthetic importance of the park was emphasized by its integration with the design of the garden. Not only could the park now be viewed from many parts of the garden: the main walks and axes of the garden were often

23 *Newburgh Priory (Yorkshire): the gardens and groves in 1744.*

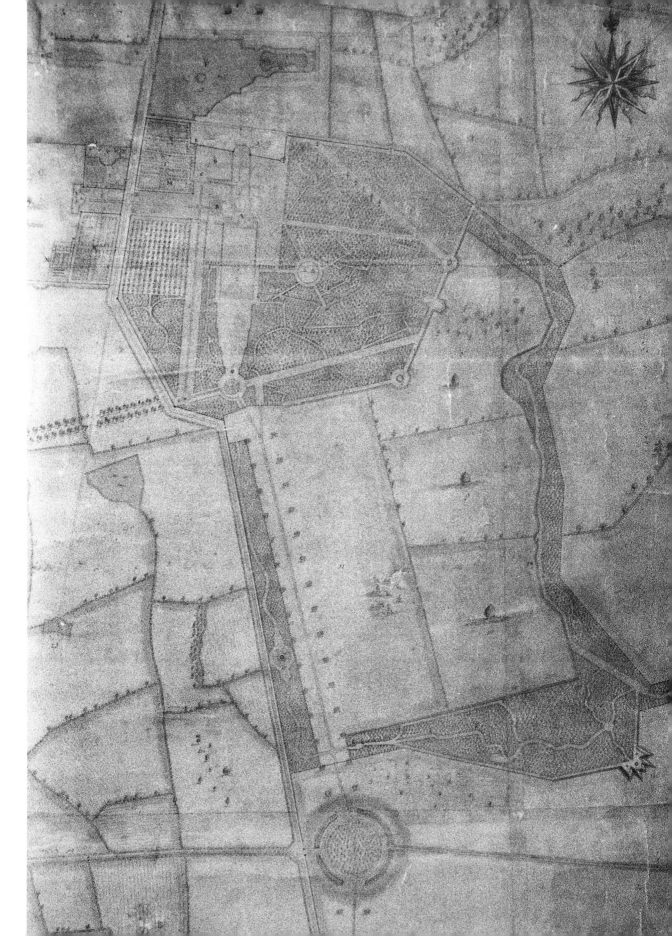

Plate I. against page 23.

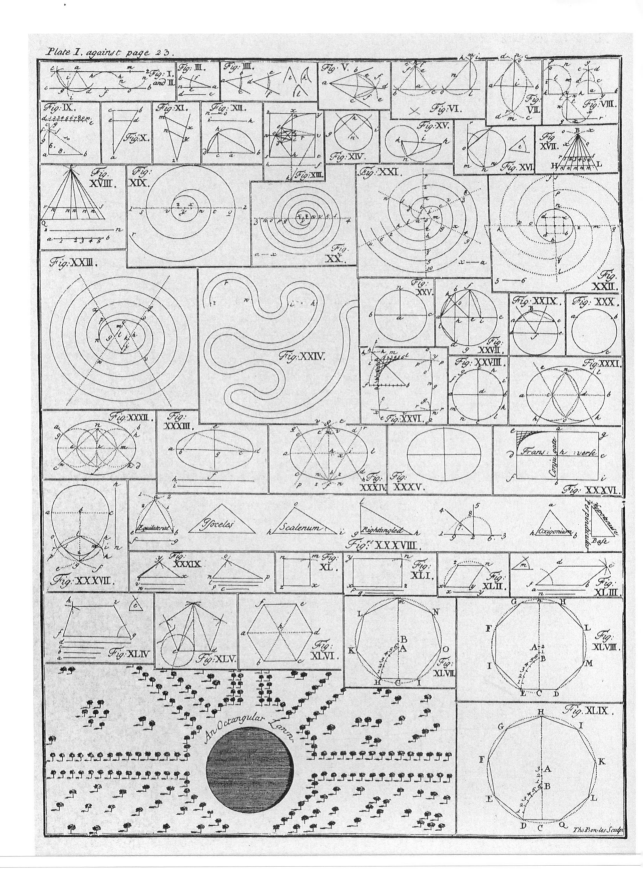

24 *The mathematics of garden design: a page from Batty Langley's* New Principles of Gardening *(1728). Figure XXIV shows the 'artinatural line'.*

extended, as avenues or vistas, far into the parkland (Fig. 25).

Parks were often extended so that the great house and its garden were surrounded by them on all sides, and insulated from the working landscape of fields and farms. Such an arrangement expressed the exclusivity of the great landowners, and their separation from the local community, just as the removal of kitchen gardens from the immediate vicinity of great houses –

something which became increasingly common from the 1720s – represented their divorce from the humdrum details of domestic production. Indeed, great pains were often taken to hide the kitchen garden from view, as at Raynham (Norfolk), where one was excavated into the side of a hill to the south of the hall.

Great gardens of this period often contained temples or other structures of classical form. Classical sculpture had been a feature of some seventeenth-century gardens, as we have seen, but temples were something new, and rather significant. From the 1710s, a group of Whig politicians consciously fostered a style of architecture which claimed to be a more faithful

25 *Houghton (Norfolk): the gardens and park, as illustrated by Colen Campbell in 1722.*

interpretation of ancient classical buildings than the confused structures which (with the exceptions of those by Inigo Jones) had characterized pre-Revolutionary elite residences, or the contemporary Baroque forms favoured by leading Tories.[10] 'Palladian' architecture – based on the ideas of the sixteenth-century architect Andrea Palladio – was vigorously promoted by Richard Boyle, Third Earl Burlington, especially through his support of the architect Colen Campbell. It was adopted for many new houses, including Robert Walpole's own home at Houghton (Norfolk). Palladianism involved strict adherence to rules – the correct combination of classical elements, the proper use of ratios – and its proponents claimed it embodied immutable, natural proportions. It was an appropriate style for the rulers of a nation claiming to be the true heir to Rome, a style superior to the Baroque of the decadent French and Spanish. Knowledge of its complex 'natural' rules (and of Renaissance and classical civilization in general) marked out the Whig elite as heirs to an ancient tradition, natural rulers of the nation.

Such ideas were also expressed in gardens, as at Chiswick, the famous garden laid out by Burlington himself.[11] Here a variety of temples were erected at nodal points in a geometric garden of canals, pleached trees, gravel walks and close-cut hedges. Similar gardens existed at a number of other places by 1725, and in the following decade many gardens could, like Castle Hill, South Molton (Devon), boast a range of classical features (in this case a pyramid, a rotunda, several obelisks, four temples and a great triumphal arch, placed at the termination of the main axial vista) (Fig. 26).[12]

To a large extent, the development of this simpler, less cluttered 'late geometric' style was related to the increase in the size of aristocratic gardens, and to the new styles of country house architecture. A proliferation of walled courts would have provided a most unsuitable setting for the clean, symmetrical lines of the Palladian house. The increased size of the gardens invited designs based on block planting and broad vistas. It would have been pointless to place such designs within a single, huge, walled enclosure, for walls were primarily intended to provide shelter and protection for plants and people, and as the size of an enclosure increased, their efficiency in doing this declined. Walls, moreover, interrupted the views out of the garden into the park, which were now being given increasing importance.

It is also possible that these larger gardens were simpler in design for economic reasons. As Stephen Switzer, writing in 1715, put it:

Gardens have gradually, insensibly, and at last even necessarily swell'd to a greater Extent than the Owner at first designed them . . .[13]

Some of the clutter may have been dispensed with simply because, in larger layouts, the maintenance costs were too great, especially

---

26 *Castle Hill, South Molton (Devon): the south view, towards the triumphal arch, still gives some impression of the grandeur of the late geometric garden.*

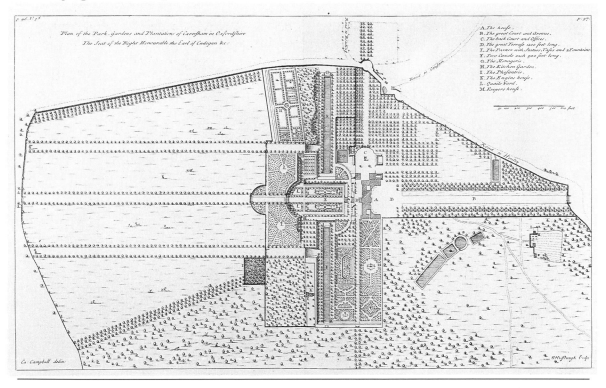

27 *Caversham (Berkshire): Stephen Switzer's great design of 1718, as illustrated in Colen Campbell's* Vitruvius Britannicus *of 1725.*

at a time when population growth was slow or non-existent and, therefore, wages were comparatively high. But this argument should not be pushed too far. The principal elements of these gardens – clipped hedges, smooth turf lawns, gravel paths – did require a large amount of maintenance. Topiary did not disappear entirely, and there were often extensive flower borders, which required regular weeding; Batty Langley advocated the planting of flowers 'in every walk'. Above all, whatever they cost to maintain, these great gardens were certainly expensive to create, not least because they often involved a great deal of earth-moving. Their aristocratic owners altered contours with an easy confidence. The garden made by Stephen Switzer for the Earl of Cadogan at Caversham near Reading is a fairly typical example (Fig. 27).

The contract for this work, dated 1718, begins by describing how Switzer is to level the area of the main parterre and raise a terrace on either side:

In which works the Borders designed for Greens and Flowers shall be well and duly prepared . . . And to be at least four foot of assize wide and two foot deep. And all such parts as are to be Grass shall be laid thereunder full four inches thick of Mold . . .[14]

The walks here, as elsewhere in the garden, were specified to be laid with gravel at least four inches thick; this completed, Switzer was to excavate two large canals on either side of the parterre, and line them with two feet of clay. Here, too, he was to make terrace walks on either side, again with borders. Next he was to make a new kitchen garden and orchard, raising the ground

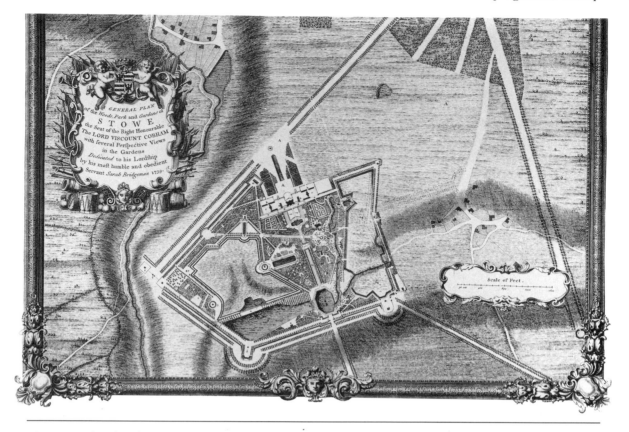

28 *Stowe (Buckinghamshire): Detail from Charles Bridgeman's magnificent design, as shown in the* Views of Stowe, *published in 1739 by his widow Sarah.*

throughout 'with Dung and mold' by between one and two feet. He was to undertake alterations to the 'new planted' walk towards Caversham, 'by abateing the riseing Ground and filling up therewith the low ground'; and he was to alter the contours around the fishponds.

It was not just levelling and earth-moving which consumed money. No expense was spared in the provision of trees, shrubs and flowers. When Switzer came to 'levell plant turf and Gravell' the wilderness, he was to use 'Forest Trees ten foot high at least'. The Earl of Cadogan was himself, by the terms of the contract, to supply many of the plants for the garden, together with the garden ornaments and a force of 160 labourers. Switzer and his team received, nevertheless,

£1392 4s 9d, a substantial sum, more than the annual income of most members of the gentry.

The 'late geometric garden' was not a static, unchanging thing. It developed in a number of ways which cannot be discussed in detail here. In particular, the 1730s saw a tendency for starker, simpler, ever larger designs, in which plantations and vistas spread ever further into the surrounding parkland, and sometimes into the agricultural land beyond. The trees in avenues were now often gathered together into clumps, and were less likely to be pleached or topiaried, and partly for this reason were increasingly planted with oak and beech, rather than lime and sweet chestnut. The later works of Charles

Bridgeman (by 1730 the leading designer for the Whig elite) display these tendencies very clearly, particularly at Stowe, designed for Lord Cobham before 1732 (Fig. 28); and Houghton, where the existing late geometric garden was extensively altered for Robert Walpole in the years around 1732 (Fig. 29, although many of the features of this design, especially the massive bastioned outer belt, were never in fact executed).[15]

The great gardens of this period have left many traces in the modern landscape. Although, as will be discussed, many were swept away to make way for more 'naturalistic' designs later in the century, a few have managed to survive in comparatively intact form, as at Bramham Park (Yorkshire), or St Pauls Waldenbury (Hertfordshire). In rather more places, the design has been extensively altered, but many of its main features, and in particular the arrangement of vistas, has been retained. Houghton (Norfolk) is a good example of this. In still more cases, only fragments have survived. There are, in particular, many extant avenues which were planted in this period. Perhaps their owners were reluctant to sacrifice a fine feature, only just maturing, on the altar of fashion as tastes changed in the second half of the century. In many places, survivals are more subtle. In particular, geometric blocks of woodland were often softened towards the end of the century, by addition and subtraction, rather than removed altogether. Careful inspection will often reveal geometric arrangements of older trees buried within later, more irregular, woodland blocks.

In addition, many of these gardens have left clear earthwork traces: examples include those designed by Bridgeman at Westbury

29 *Houghton (Norfolk): Bridgeman's design for the grounds, published by Isaac Ware in 1735. The plan, which was to replace the layout shown in Fig. 25, was only partially executed.*

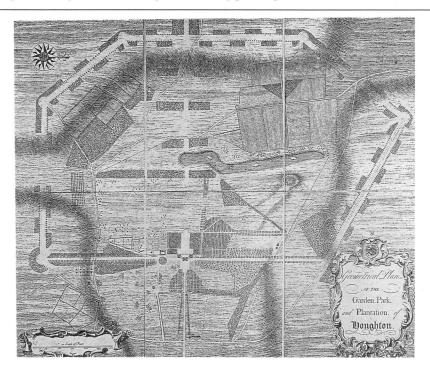

(Hampshire) and Eastbury (Dorset).[16] Sometimes, as at Wanstead (Essex), earthworks survive together with remnants of the original planting. Similarly, at Gunton (Norfolk), the massive viewing mound designed by Bridgeman stands in an ornamental grove containing many of the trees originally planted in the 1730s. A careful survey by Jon Phibbs has revealed the planting layout; the straight walks were edged with beech, the compartments between them were composed largely of sweet chestnut and oak. The design is currently being restored.

The sheer scale of these landscapes meant that extensive schemes of earth-moving – to open up vistas or make way for avenues – were often carried out far beyond the confines of the garden itself. At Althorp in (Northamptonshire), a low spur some 400m (1300ft) to the south of the house was sharply truncated by the Spencer family in the 1730s, to allow the passage of an avenue.[17] At Houghton (Norfolk), in the following decade, a massive cutting was made through the hill to the east of the hall, to open up a vista. Work was abandoned, uncompleted, on the death of Robert Walpole in 1745, and the cutting has, in consequence, a somewhat irregular appearance, with piles of spoil apparently grassed over *in situ* as tree mounds. This phenomenal project is referred to in a single, undated memorandum in the estate archives, which – to us – says much about the practice of aristocratic gardening in this fascinating period:

Item: the matter of removing the hill to be decided.

Alternatives to geometry

Thus it was that the great geometric gardens dramatically symbolized the power of the Whig oligarchs, and it is not surprising that their political opponents made vocal criticisms of the 'vanity of expense' involved in their creation. The prominent poet and essayist Alexander Pope – who created his own famous, if idiosyncratic, garden at Twickenham – was one critic, although his position was slightly ambivalent.[18] He was a Catholic and a Tory, yet also a member of Burlington's circle and a friend of Bridgeman. In his *Epistle to Burlington* he praised Bridgeman's design at Stowe, and Burlington's buildings at Chiswick. But in his description of the mythical 'Timon's Villa' he ridiculed the more ostentatious and predictable features of the late geometric garden:

Grove nods at grove, each Alley has a brother
And half the platform just reflects the other.[19]

It was not only the expense which offended, but also the divorce of these gardens from the working countryside. Not surprising, then, that some prominent Tory politicians like Viscount Bolingbroke and Henry Bathurst consciously adopted a form of gardening which mixed the practical and aesthetic, thereby displaying their solidarity with the broad mass of the local gentry. Bolingbroke, returning from political exile in 1725 to Dawley in Middlesex, established a simple garden with a mesh of avenues radiating out through the surrounding farmland; while at Richings, some 16km (10 miles) away, Bathurst planted a wilderness in which the quarters contained areas 'for sowing of Corn, Turnips etc and for feeding of Cattle'.[20]

As early as 1713 Joseph Addison had argued:

Why may not a whole Estate be thrown into a kind of Garden, by frequent Plantations, that may turn as much to the Profitt as the Pleasure of the Owner? . . . a Man might make a pretty Landscape of his own Possessions.[21]

Such ideas were given a comprehensive expression by Stephen Switzer in his

Nobleman, Gentleman, and Gardeners Recreation, published in 1715, which became the first part of his larger work, *Ichnographia Rustica*, in 1718.[22] Although in his actual commissions, like Caversham, Switzer worked firmly in the prevailing late geometric idiom, in these works he advocated a form of 'rural or extensive' gardening. The main axes of a small and relatively simple 'inner garden' should, he argued, be extended as rides and avenues through working farmland 'as far as Liberty of Planting will allow', so that the whole would 'appear as a part, and add to the Beauty and Magnificence of the Garden in the View, tho' not in the Expense of Keeping'.[23] Switzer had some association with leading Tories, and the second edition of *Ichnographia Rustica* contined a description of Richings and Dawley which Switzer described by the term *la ferme ornée*, or ornamental farm.

The connection between garden design and politics must not be overstated – Switzer's recipe for affordable magnificence would have appealed to a small landowner of whatever political persuasion. Moreover, the differences between this 'extensive gardening' and the more normal late geometric gardens of the period should not be exaggerated. With their straight avenues and vistas focusing on the house, each represented variations on the same geometric theme. In fact, the basic principles of the late geometric style only began to be challenged, and then only at a few places and in a very limited way, during the middle and late 1730s.

At this time, the principal opposition to Walpole's dominance came from a group of disaffected Whigs, the 'Boy Patriots', who were associated with the household of George II's son, Frederick, Prince of Wales. Frederick's own garden at Carleton House in London was redesigned around 1733 by William Kent, who up to this time had been involved in painting, architecture, interior decoration and the design of garden buildings. In the same year Kent's main patron, Burlington, resigned from Walpole's administration during a famous dispute over excise duty. By the end of the year, Kent was busy altering his gardens at Chiswick. Lord Cobham also resigned over the Excise Bill, and by 1734 Kent was at work at Stowe. In the same year Sir Thomas Robinson wrote:

There is a new taste in gardening just arisen, which has been practised with so great success at the Prince's garden in Town, that a general alteration of some of the most considerable gardens in the Kingdom is begun, after Mr Kent's notion of gardening, viz, to lay them out, and work without line or level . . . The celebrated gardens at Claremont, Chiswick, and Stowe are full of labourers, to modernise the expensive works finished in them, ever since everyone's memory.[24]

What was different about these gardens? At Stowe, Kent created a new, highly irregular compartment within Bridgeman's vast geometric design, called the 'Elysian Fields'. This had a 'serpentine river' and irregularly-planted trees. There were no hedges here, or straight gravelled paths, but there was a remarkable collection of buildings which formed a series of framed 'pictures', and which conveyed strong philosophical and political messages in their location, design, dedications and inscriptions.[25] Thus the Temple of Modern Virtue was a ruin which contained a headless statue, said to represent Walpole, while the 'Gothic Temple', a castle-like structure, was probably a reference to the (largely mythical) democratic system of the Saxons and other ancient Germanic tribes. Similar gothic buildings now appeared alongside the more normal classical ones in other gardens of this new, irregular type being created by members of Frederick's household: at Hagley, for example, laid out from the 1740s by George Lyttleton, the Prince's principal secretary;[26] at Wroxton Abbey (Oxfordshire), created by the Earl of Guildford;[27] and, most notably of all, at Painshill (Sussex), on a site laid out from 1738 around a 12ha (30 acre) lake by Charles Hamilton.[28]

The last two gardens also included Chinese buildings, and at Painshill there was a 'Turkish Tent', and these too may have had an ideological significance, the former referring to the supposed virtues of the Chinese political system (about which, in reality, nobody knew very much at all). But for the most part these romantic structures were simply meant to be enjoyed for their emotional effects, for the feelings of melancholy or romance that they inspired, and this is why such gardens became popular. They represented a rejection of the ideas which had underpinned the enthusiasm for Palladianism in the previous decades. Beauty was not simply to be thought of as the inevitable consequence of ideal 'natural' forms. It resided in the experience of the observer, and was therefore, to some extent, in the eye of the beholder. It was a system of aesthetics at once more individual, and less deferential.

Another important feature of these gardens was the great diversity of trees, shrubs and flowers planted within them. Thus at Painshill, Hamilton planted a phenomenal range of exotic conifers, and the first American rhododendrons to be established in England. Flowering shrubs of diverse kinds were planted throughout the gardens. Similarly, at Rousham (Oxfordshire) in 1750, the garden laid out by William Kent was said to contain 'a greater veriaty of evergreens, and Flowering Shrubs, then you can possably see in any one walk in the World'.[29] To some extent, gardens of all kinds were more diversely planted than in the previous century. Increasing numbers of nurseries were marketing increasing numbers of new hardy introductions, especially from the British

colonies in North America: the 1724 catalogue of the London nurseryman Robert Furber lists nearly 400 varieties of trees and shrubs alone.[30] But these new irregular gardens seem to have used a greater range of plants, and used them more extensively, than was usual in contemporary gardens of late geometric form.

The most important feature of gardens like Painshill, Wroxton, or Hagley, however, was that they were no longer primarily organized around great linear vistas focusing on the house. Instead, the various experiences and 'pictures' offered by the complex planting and the buildings, and by the views out beyond the confines of the garden, were laid out along a circuit walk. Even if a number of possible routes existed, there often seems to have been one 'correct' way of negotiating the garden, which presented the sites, objects, views or scenes in the proper order.

A letter written in 1750 by John MacClary, the gardener at Rousham, describes in detail the 'undulating walk' which is the 'way to view' the garden.[31] Rousham is a fairly small garden, covering no more than 7ha (17 acres), although this is hardly apparent in Kent's clever design, which uses distant views to a gothic eyecatcher, and a particularly devious circuit walk. Indeed, this new style was eminently suitable for the grounds of a comparatively small 'villa' residence – the country house of a London financier, merchant or government official. The use of a circular winding walk allowed the real size of a garden to be obscured, while the inclusion within the design of framed views beyond the garden itself made it possible to borrow, as it were, the aesthetic features in the landscapes of surrounding owners. Moreover, many of the characteristic garden buildings (especially the Chinese and 'rustic' structures) could be constructed of wood, at comparatively little expense.

The style could also be easily adapted into

the *ferme ornée* tradition. Men of small means but with cultivated taste, made elaborate, ribbon-like gardens with numerous seats, classical urns and inscriptions, running through working farms, carefully using framed views of the more picturesque elements of the countryside, and screening out the less acceptable aspects. Thus Philip Southcote used the money gained from his marriage in 1733 to the 67-year-old Duchess of Cleveland to lay out Woburn farm, a particularly famous example of this type of gardening.[32] The Leasowes, created from 1745 by William Shenstone in Warwickshire, included views of the local hills (the Wrekin, Frankley Beeches) and a number of bridges, cascades, urns, a grotto as well as the picturesque ruins of a priory.[33]

Small gardens in the new serpentine style attracted much ribald criticism. Francis Coventry, writing in the journal *The World*, parodied 'Squire Mushroom' who turned a farmhouse into a villa and laid out gardens of less than two acres, with:

... a yellow serpentine river, stagnating through a beautiful valley, which extends near twenty yards in length.[34]

The impact of these irregular gardens on the present landscape is very limited. In part, this is because they relied for their effects on plants with a relatively short life-span, and on buildings which were, in most cases, insubstantial.

Hamilton's Painshill is currently being restored, and is well worth a visit. So too is Rousham, where much has survived, mainly because Kent's buildings are of stone. Wroxton's fate is more typical. Here the Chinese buildings and the Chinese bridge, have all disappeared (they were of wood) but the stone Gothic dovecot survives, while the cascade at the head of the serpentine river is being reconstructed.

The survival of geometry

The main reason why these irregular gardens have left little trace on the English landscape is that they were rare. Most garden historians talk a lot about those texts published in the 1760s which popularized the new, irregular gardens: books like William Shenstone's rather aptly-titled *Unconnected Thoughts on Gardening* (1764) and George Mason's *An Essay on Design in Gardening* (1768). But more numerous in the studies and libraries of the gentry were books like Henry Stevenson's *The Gentleman Gardener's Recreation*. First published in 1716, it was reprinted in its eleventh edition in 1764, this time 'considerably improved by the Addition of . . . a complete Kalandar, shewing what Work is to be done every Month in the Yaer'. In January, the gentleman gardener was advised to 'Prune up wilderness trees, and flowering shrubs where they grow too much out of shape; dig up the ground in the quarters . . .'. In February, he was reminded to break up and turn gravel walks, rake and clean the wilderness quarters, and 'Plant Dutch Box Edgings to Borders'. In July, he was to 'Cut and trim Hedges, clip Box-edgings, mow Grass-plats, and keep the Walks constantly rolled'. Texts like this clearly assumed a style of gardening little different from that practised in the early decades of the century.

It is true that certain elements of the new, irregular, serpentine gardens were widely adopted during the 1740s and 1750s by the aristocracy and gentry. In particular, the rich and varied planting evident at gardens like Painshill, to some extent, appeared in all gardens. This, plus the widespread adoption of serpentine walks, meant that the wilderness of earlier decades gradually developed into, and was increasingly referred to as, the shrubbery. But the overall structure of most gardens remained strongly geometric and symmetrical, organized, not

30 *Mid-Hertfordshire in the 1760s. This detail from Drury and Andrew's map of 1766 shows the wide variety of geometric styles current in the middle decades of the eighteenth century.*

on a circuit walk, but around avenues or vistas focusing on the main facade of the house. Thus when, in 1743, Sir Nicholas Carver was considering alterations to the gardens at Beddington (Berkshire), the main question was 'how to preserve the Simetry and take away some part of the Expense'.[35]

Evidence from maps and illustrations suggests that well into the second half of the century, most residences were surrounded by some form of geometric garden, even in the more fashionable areas of the country,

near to the metropolis, such as Hertfordshire. Here, a map of the county surveyed in the 1760s, and published in 1766, shows most of the great houses with their gardens still, essentially, in the 'late geometric' style, and with parks tightly packed with radiating avenues and vistas (Fig. 30). It also shows many more modest

31 *Kendals, Aldenham (Hertfordshire): a fine example of a mid-eighteenth-century garden design.*

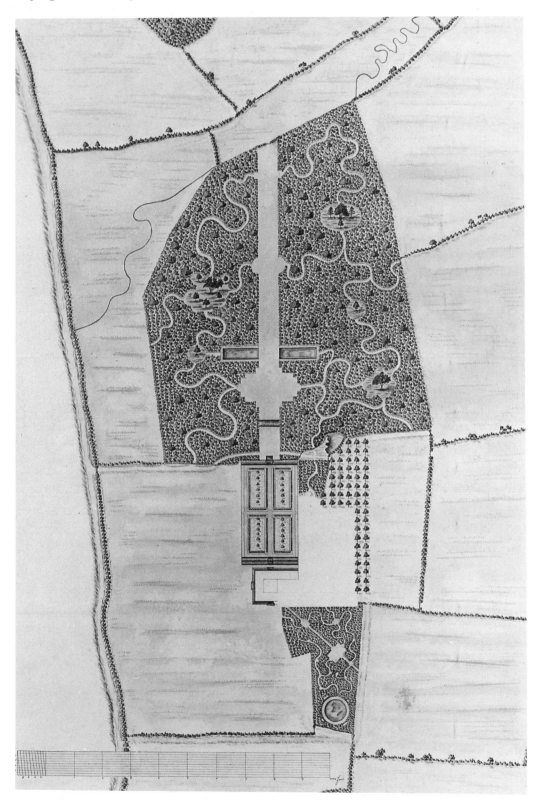

arrangements, involving walled enclosures and geometric pleasure grounds.[36] Estate maps from the area provide more details about such gardens. A plan of Kendals in Aldenham, undated but probably drawn up in the 1750s, shows that the main garden area, next to the house, was walled, and contained geometric flower beds (Fig. 31).[37] But beyond stretched a vast wilderness, with serpentine paths, planted on either side of a broad walk focusing on the main facade of the house; half way along its length was a geometric pond. The walled courts have gone, but the pond survives, together with the remnants of the 'wilderness', in the grounds of a private school. Massive coppices of hornbeam and sweet chestnut, together with a characteristic ground flora, make it clear that the 'wilderness' was, in fact, a pre-existing ancient wood, adapted as a pleasure ground in true Switzerian fashion.

Even in areas close to fashionable London, therefore, most country house gardens in the 1760s and 1770s were still, essentially, of geometric form. So, too, were those of the larger urban houses, in market towns and cities.[38] And deep in the countryside, in Northumberland, Northamptonshire or Norfolk, the gardens of the rural squirearchy were even more traditional. Within their walled enclosures, as in previous centuries, aesthetic and practical planting might be thoroughly mixed, and areas of more irregular shrubbery planting were usually absent, or of negligible importance. Even the bold sweeps of the 'late geometric' style had largely passed such gardens by.

It was not simply that the local gentry lacked the means to do something more fashionable. It is clear, from an examination of surviving walled gardens, that money could be found for their alteration, and even

extension, well into the second half of the century. It was simply that local squires often lacked the inclination to change. Their gardens expressed different needs, and a different lifestyle, to those of the great aristocrats, fashionable London merchants or educated dilettantes. Art historians often give the impression that the eighteenth-century landowner was interested, above all, in poetry, painting and philosophy. In reality, most gentlemen were predominantly concerned with planting things and killing things. Their diaries and memoranda books show them busy with details of estate administration, with their home farms, with brewing, with the establishment of plantations, with hunting, with the management of fishponds and dovehouses – and with the care of their gardens. We see them buying plants and seeds from the growing network of provincial nurseries, exchanging cuttings with their neighbours, pruning fruit trees and planting vegetables. The garden was one arena for a lifestyle which was devoted to the virtues of domestic production on a country estate. As long as the provincial gentry extolled the virtues of rural life, so long did the garden maintain its dominant position in front of the main facades of the house.

Gardens in the middle decades of the eighteenth century displayed a rich variety of styles, although almost all were geometric in form. Yet already, in the 1760s, this diversity was beginning to be eroded by the adoption of a single, shared style; and by 1800, the houses of all with any pretension to gentry status were set free of gardens, and stood in the wide, sweeping, irregular landscape of the park. How this happened, and why, will be investigated in the next chapter.

4 The landscape park

Brown and his 'imitators'

The landscape park is so familiar – surrounded as we are by hundreds, in various states of decay – that its basic form hardly needs description. It was an irregular, 'natural' landscape of grass and scattered indigenous trees, together with some larger clumps and plantations. The whole ensemble was usually surrounded, in whole or part, by a perimeter belt (Figs 32 and 33). Where an owner had the money and the

32 *Sandon (Staffordshire): vertical aerial photograph of a typical landscape park. Note the traces of ridge and furrow, bottom centre; the detached kitchen garden, top centre; and the perimeter belts.*

33 *Blickling (Norfolk): typical English parkland landscape, with lake and scattered trees.*

terrain was amenable, the design often included a serpentine lake. The house stood free of gardens and walled courts, and the parkland swept right up to the principal facades – or at least, appeared to do so. In reality, an area of mown lawn lay immediately adjacent to the mansion, divided from the park by a discrete ha-ha. The kitchen garden was hidden: either tucked away behind the stable block, or lost in the distant recesses of the park.[1]

The traditional explanation for this new kind of landscape is quite straightforward. It was initially invented by Lancelot 'Capability' Brown, and then widely copied; and it represented the culmination of the development towards an increasingly irregular, 'naturalistic' landscape supposedly pioneered by Switzer, Bridgeman and Kent.[2]

Lancelot Brown certainly has had a major impact on the English landscape. Beginning as a gardener in Northumberland, he moved south in 1739, and by 1741 was employed by Lord Cobham at Stowe, where he was largely involved in the execution of Kent's designs. Even while at Stowe he was occasionally 'lent out' by his employer, to friends and associates. In 1751, soon after Cobham's death, he moved to the outskirts of London and set up in business. By the end of the decade, he had worked on some twenty landed estates. But it was in the following decades that his business really took off, and when he died in 1783 he had been involved in perhaps 170 major commissions.[3]

Brown was a brilliant and successful designer, but it is necessary to see his life, like the lives of all 'great men', in proper context. To begin with, it is worth stating what was *not* original about Brown's style. Firstly, he did not, single-handedly, invent the irregular, 'natural' scenery of the park. This, as we have seen, had long been a landscape of immense cultural significance. In previous chapters the progressive rise in its importance as a setting for the country house has been followed, and it is hard to overemphasize the debt owed by the landscape park to the traditional deer park, or, indeed, the degree of continuity between them.[4] Many great 'landscape parks' developed directly out of, and continued in part to function as, deer parks, especially in areas like Hertfordshire or Buckinghamshire, where they had long been particularly common. Most of Brown's creations fall into this category, for his patrons were, for the most part, the kinds of wealthy aristocrats who would inevitably have possessed a deer park next to their homes. In such cases, Brown simply modified the existing landscape, paying particular attention to the immediate vicinity of the house – where the old gardens were swept away – and to the middle distance – where a serpentine lake was usually created, often through the adaptation of an existing system of canals or basins. Only a few of Brown's creations were true *landscape* parks, in the sense that they never contained deer.

Secondly, it is worth stressing that the

idea of the *landscape* park, as opposed to the deer park, was not entirely new. Already, by the 1720s and 1730s, some gentry houses had, outside their gardens, areas which were called 'parks', and which had the irregular, naturalistic appearance of the deer park, but which never seem to have contained deer.[5] These had something of the ancient, aristocratic aura of the true park, yet their owners avoided all the expenses involved in the maintenance of a herd of deer.

Lastly, to see Brown in his proper context, it must not be forgotten that, in spite of his prodigious output, he created only a tiny minority of the landscape parks of England.[6] Most were designed by nameless local gardeners, land agents, or the owners themselves, but many others were created by designers like Nathaniel Richmond, William Emes and Richard Woods, working on large numbers of commissions over quite wide areas of the country.[7] Unlike most of Brown's works, these were true landscape parks in the sense that they were entirely new creations, made at the expense of agricultural and and never for deer. Humphry Repton, writing at the end of the century, could be scathing about the designs created by Brown's contemporaries.

It seems as if Landscape Gardening was so easy, that every Land Surveyor thinks himself competent to deliver an Opinion in that Art.[8]

---

34 *Little Linford (Buckinghamshire): Richard Wood's design for the park and pleasure-grounds, 1763. The house looks out across open parkland, but to the east there is an elaborate pleasure ground, laid out around a long narrow lake.*

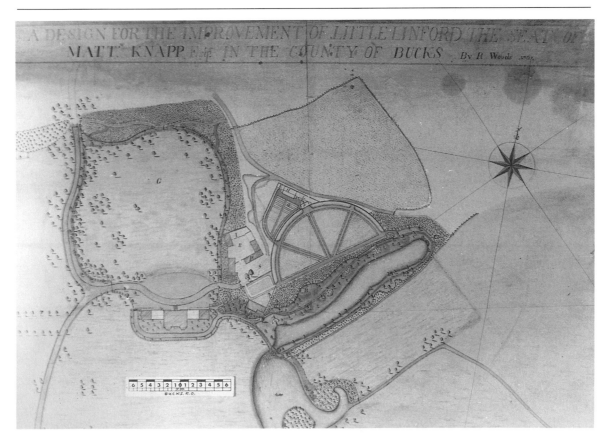

For the most part, later historians have concurred in seeing even men like Emes, Richmond and Woods as mere 'imitators' of the great Brown. But this is almost certainly a considerable over-simplification. To some extent, Brown looms so large in the history of garden design simply because of the importance of his clients. He was not alone in forging the pace, or pattern, of stylistic change. The designs created by a wide group of men, including Brown, developed in parallel, through the 1750s and 1760s.

Their early work had much in common with that of William Kent and other designers of the 1740s: that is, views across open parkland were given increasing prominence, but elaborate pleasure grounds, with circuit walks, serpentine paths, shrubberies and garden buildings, were still important. Thus, for example, Brown's design for Petworth (Sussex) in 1751 included an elaborate garden containing a classical 'Rotunda' and a Doric temple (reused from the existing garden), together with a wide range of flowers and flowering shrubs, including butcher's broom, honeysuckle, spirea, lilac and acacia. There were gardens for aloes and bay trees, plantations of evergreens and a cypress walk.[9] Richard Wood's plan for Little Linford (Buckinghamshire) (Fig. 34) is typical, combining as it does a parkland setting for the main facade of the house, with an elaborate pleasure ground, including temples and gothic buildings, to one side of the main vista.

Only gradually did these more artificial, architectural, 'Kentian' elements decline in importance, and what we now think of as the characteristically 'Brownian' aspects come to the fore; the rolling turf of the open park, the clumps and the irregular scatter of trees. Already, in the late 1750s, Francis Richardson was preparing plans for places in Yorkshire in which the pleasure ground was small and marginalized, with the house standing in a landscape of uncluttered 'natural' simplicity.[10] But it was not until the end of the following decade that this simple parkland style began to catch on.

By the 1780s, landscape parks were becoming a common feature of the landscape. But they were always more common in some areas than in others. Fig. 35, plotting the distribution of late eighteenth-century parks in eastern England, shows this well. Small and medium-sized parks tended to cluster around major urban centres (note the 'packing' around Norwich, and in the south of Essex, towards London).[11] Many people of wealth and culture preferred, all things being equal, to live within easy distance of the shops and entertainments which such centres provided. Successful businessmen similarly built houses with small parks within easy reach of their place of work. Other areas, in contrast, were characterized by small numbers of large parks. These were usually areas dominated by arable farming, especially those where the land was of fairly poor quality. It was in such regions that very large estates had, by the end of the eighteenth century, come to dominate the landholding pattern. This explains (referring again to Fig. 35) the relative absence of small and medium-sized parks in north-west Norfolk, where most of the land was owned by the Cokes of Holkham, the Townshends of Raynham, and the Walpoles of Houghton.

Some areas had few parks of any kind. These were often areas of particularly fertile soils, or of mainly pastoral agriculture, where small freehold farms continued to flourish, and where large estates were comparatively few in number. Hence the paucity of parks on the central claylands of

35 *The distribution of landscape parks in eastern England, c.1790.*

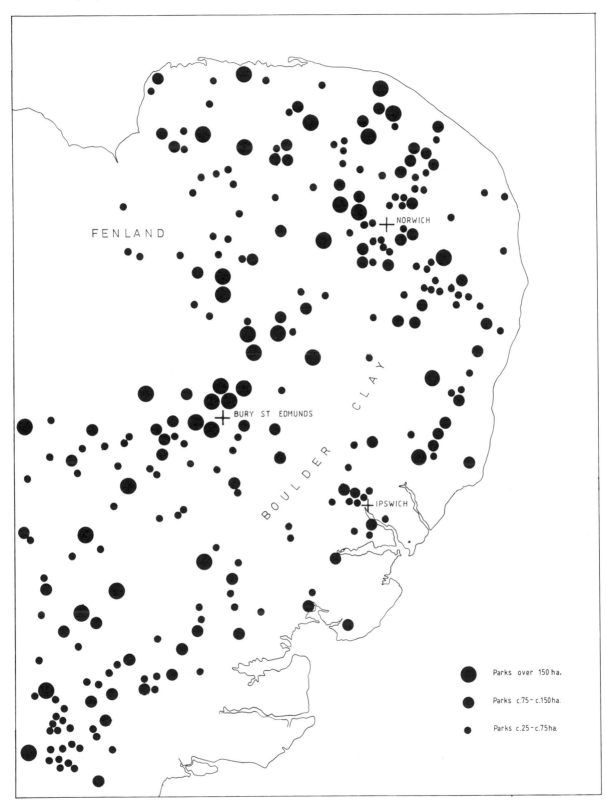

FENLAND

NORWICH

BOULDER CLAY

BURY ST EDMUNDS

IPSWICH

Parks over 150 ha.

Parks c.75 – c.150ha.

Parks c.25 – c.75ha.

East Anglia, and in the Fenlands, although in the latter case the flat and uninspiring appearance of the landscape also made it an unpopular place for the rich to make their homes. In these and other ways, the distribution of parks in the later eighteenth century was closely bound up with patterns of land ownership, and with the social lives and aesthetic preferences of their creators.

The density of parks in eastern England is not typical of the country as a whole, although the factors behind their distribution here were probably important everywhere. There were, for example, rather fewer parks in Devon or Cornwall, or in Sussex, because of the distance of these places from major urban centres, and the survival here into the nineteenth century of large numbers of small freehold farmers. In general, wherever large landowners were thick on the ground, so too were landscape parks. On the other hand, Fig. 35 is, perhaps, slightly misleading, in that it is not always entirely clear what contemporaries meant when they used the term 'park' on maps or in documents. At the lower end of the market, some 'parks' differed only in degree from the working agricultural landscape, and merely consisted of one or two large fields put down to pasture in the immediate vicinity of the mansion, with some ornamental planting. Many of these smaller 'parks' may thus have been omitted from the county maps on which this illustration is based. If we could include all these omissions, the map would be even more crowded with dots, and would express even more clearly its most important message: that, by the end of the eighteenth century, the landscape park had become the quintessential symbol of gentility.

Why was this? Why did the landscape park become so popular with landowners, who, after all, paid their money and took their choice? While Brown and his more famous 'imitators' may, or may not, have been great artists, they were certainly, for

the most part, good businessmen, providing clients with landscapes they felt they wanted. Brown himself ended up as a landowner in his own right, and High Sheriff of Huntingdonshire – not bad for someone who had started his career in the kitchen garden. In part, the enthusiasm for the park was connected with changes in philosophical ideas, and with the development of new attitudes to nature on the part of landowners. With the progressive enclosure of common land, there were fewer and fewer areas of irregular, natural landscape left in England. Nature had been controlled, and could now be admitted into the private grounds of the landowners, if suitably dressed and tamed. But more importantly, these new landscapes were popular because they answered a number of pressing needs on the part of the social groups who paid for them.

The context of the park

The second half of the eighteenth century saw the first phases of the Industrial Revolution under way. In the north and west of England, towns like Birmingham and Manchester grew in size, and canals spread through the landscape. But change was also occurring in rural areas. The population began to grow again, and by the end of the century it was increasing rapidly. This, coupled with the impact of the Napoleonic Wars, meant that agricultural prices, and therefore farm rents, also rose quickly. Together with a gradual shift in the burden of taxation away from land and on to consumables, this meant that the second half of the eighteenth century saw an increase in the wealth and importance of the local gentry. This period also saw what has been called the 'Consumer Revolution', the development of a society increasingly geared towards the consumption of mass-produced, fashionable items.[11] A glance at any eighteenth-century newspaper will demonstrate the vast range of clothes, medicines, books, services and entertainments on offer in the provincial towns.

The great geometric gardens of the early eighteenth century had been appropriate to a rural and hierarchical society, in which the power of great landowners was displayed with pride and arrogance; a society which had differed only in degree from the absolutist monarchies of continental Europe. But increasingly, as the century progressed, the ruling elite chose to emphasize a different way of life, often referred to as 'polite society'.[12] Differences of rank between the great landowners and the broad mass of the local gentry, and the wealthier professionals, were consciously played down. Instead, emphasis was placed on contact without constraint between members of these groups, regardless of occupation or background. The arrogance of the nobility, the ignorance of the backwood's squire, the ideological motivation ('enthusiasm') of the Jacobite or the Puritan, were all anathema to this wider, easy-going, consumer-orientated ruling group, as they rubbed shoulders amicably at Bath, or in the Assembly Rooms of the provincial towns. Gardens of naked grandeur were increasingly unnecessary and inappropriate in this new, more complex society.

The smaller geometric gardens around the homes of the lesser gentry were also unsuited to this different world. As their owners flourished, and grew closer culturally to the great landowners, they also drew away from their neighbours in the local community. They had less and less in common with their tenant farmers and the local freeholders. Direct 'hands on' involvement in the details of estate and domestic management, and in gardening, now seemed to smack of the lifestyle of their less exalted neighbours. Such things were increasingly shunned by the local squire, and gardens were seen more and more as an inappropriate setting for a polite residence.

At the same time, members of the local gentry were gaining land, and consolidating their estates, as new agricultural techniques and market forces pushed many small freeholders into liquidation. This development was also encouraged by the enclosure of open fields and commons, which was proceeding apace at this time.[13] Local landowners were now in a position to emulate the parkland setting of the houses of the very rich. In addition, they had a particular need to do so. Numerous references in literature, correspondence and diaries make it clear that the local poor were increasingly regarded as a problem, even a threat, as population growth outstripped employment possibilities. The plight of the rural poor was made worse by the enclosure of common land, which often removed from them a vital safety-net against indigence.[14]

Increasingly, landowners simply turned their backs on the whole mess, retreating into a safe, pastoral, 'natural' landscape, one which gave them seclusion and privacy, and which at the same time expressed their cultural identity with the greatest landowners. It was in this search for social segregation that the park made (and arguably, still makes) its greatest contribution to the English landscape.

The park in the landscape

Many of the designed landscapes of the first half of the eighteenth century had incorporated wide views across the adjacent countryside. Often, as at Rousham, distant eye-catchers had been purpose-built to draw the eye across the intervening fields, but sometimes it was pre-existing features which formed the focus for views and vistas. In the late eighteenth and early nineteenth centuries, things changed. Views beyond the perimeter were now less important than those within, and parks were increasingly hemmed in by belts of trees. Brown and his contemporaries may have removed walls from around the house, but the belt encircling the park often became, in Repton's words, a boundary 'scarce less offensive than the pale'. As a result, many parks are rather self-contained landscapes, and today impinge on the surrounding environment through their external belts. The impact of these can still be tremendous, especially in the predominantly arable areas of eastern England, which have suffered most in the last four decades from the destruction of woods and hedgerows.

Another, more dramatic, manifestation of the search for privacy was the destruction and relocation of settlements. The village shifted by the local lord to make way for his park is a powerful image.

Have we not seen, at Pleasure's lordly call
The smiling, long-frequented village fall?
Behold the duteous son, the sire decay'd
The modest matron, and the blushing maid,
Forced from their homes, a melancholy train
To traverse climes beyond the western main.[15]

– as Goldsmith wrote in 1777. Many readers will have heard of Milton Abbas, a large settlement – almost a small town – destroyed and rebuilt on the fringes of Milton Abbey park in 1765; or Nuneham Courtenay in Oxfordshire, removed by Lord Harcourt in the 1760s.[16] Village clearance, however, was largely restricted to the greatest estates, for only the very rich usually owned sizeable settlements lock, stock and barrel, and could afford the extravagance of demolishing a village, and (often) of providing a purpose-built, 'model', replacement. Many clearances were thus associated with the creation or expansion of deer parks in the seventeenth and early eighteenth centuries, rather than with the establishment of landscape parks in

36 *Houghton (Norfolk): the earthworks of the deserted settlement, and associated features, in the north park.*

the late eighteenth. Examples of village clearance can, it is true, be found in most counties, but there are only a handful in each. Total destruction of villages was most common in the Midlands, where the pattern of settlement was most strongly nucleated. Here the manor house usually stood within a village, with houses clustering around. Their removal might be necessary if a park was to be laid out. Even here, however, the number of emparked settlements was probably low. In Northamptonshire, for example, between 1720 and 1850 only eight villages were entirely destroyed, although a further 25 had their form significantly altered to make way for parks.[17] Elsewhere the figures are much lower. In Norfolk – an area with a more dispersed pattern of settlement – no more than five or six villages were destroyed by emparking.

These numbers may sound surprisingly low, for there are indeed many examples of deserted settlement sites in parks. A detailed survey in Hampshire, for example, has revealed that as many as half the parks in the county contain archaeological evidence for abandoned settlements.[18] But the relationship between such sites, and the parks within which they lie, is frequently subtle and complex. Parks often contain the traces of settlements which had disappeared long before the park was laid out, because both settlement desertion, and emparking, are separate manifestations of strong, resident lordship. Where settlements dwindled to nothing, or were intentionally depopulated, during the demographic and economic changes of the late medieval period, the manor house would often survive, accompanied by one or two farms. If, much later, the lord of the manor laid out

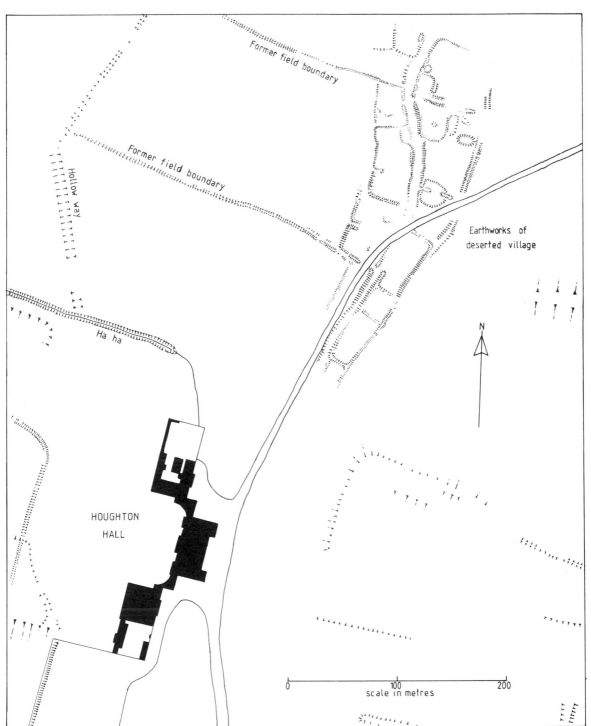

a park around his residence, it would often incorporate the earthwork traces of the former village. On the other hand, settlements which fell under the control of a single landowner during the medieval period, or later, often declined in size drastically during the seventeenth and eighteenth centuries, due to the workings of the Elizabethan Poor Law.[19] The principal proprietors and tenants in a community were responsible for paying the poor rate, and so a sole owner often worked to reduce the size of the village, in order to limit the number of people who, through poverty, infirmity or old age, were likely to be claimants for poor relief.

Nineteenth-century commentators talked much about the distinction between such 'closed' parishes, and the sprawling, uncontrolled 'open' parishes, where ownership of property was more spread. But the distinction was already manifest in the seventeenth century, and Sir Roger North, writing in the 1690s, was able to describe how:

Gentlemen of late years have taken up an Humour of Destroying their Tenements and Cottages, whereby they make it impossible that mankind should inhabit upon their estates. This is done sometimes barefaced, because they harbour the Poor that are a charge to the Parish.[20]

Settlement remains within parks are, therefore, often the result of desertion which took place before the parks themselves were established. Indeed, where settlements were cleared away to make way for parks, they had usually already declined in size.

Houghton (Norfolk) is a good example. The village is first shown on a map of 1719, lying on the southern fringes of the park. By the early 1730s, it had been removed to allow for the southwards expansion of the park, and a model estate village, New Houghton, was built some 500m (1600ft) to the south as a replacement. The church of St Martin was left isolated within the park, but virtually no earthwork traces of the village can be seen. However, to the north of the hall, within the area already emparked by 1719, extensive earthworks mark an earlier extension of the village, along a long north-south street (Fig. 36). This arm of the village had almost certainly disappeared before

the park was first laid out, in the later seventeenth century. Because it was already long-abandoned, it was not subjected to the same kind of systematic levelling as the southern part of the village.

Although destruction of entire villages might have been rare, even quite minor local squires relocated individual farms and cottages which lay in the path of their new landscapes; unlike the more dramatic clearances of entire villages, these minor adjustments to the pattern of settlement continued into the second half of the nineteenth century. Maps and field surveys, reveal many examples. But far more common than this was the diversion or termination of public rights-of-way – roads, tracks or footpaths – which almost always occurred when parks were laid out. There are numerous examples, in every county, of roads which suddenly veer off course as park walls, or the park gate, are approached. As mentioned in the introduction, the legislation of 1773 made it much easier and cheaper to close or divert roads. All that was required was the agreement of two county magistrates, men from the same social group as the applicant and, as often as not, neighbours or friends. Road closure orders make amusing reading, for they always maintain the polite fiction that the proposed change is for the general public good. A road to be closed or diverted is always superfluous to requirements, an unnecessary burden on the parish, or inconvenient in some way, while a replacement is of better quality and more direct. But the real reason for the change is sometimes implied. In 1788, T. W. Coke closed a road to the west of Holkham park, to allow for its expansion. A new road, 'more commodious', had already been completed (this was often the case, and an indication, if one were needed, that no effective opposition to the change was expected). This was in 'good condition and repair and fit for the passage of his majesty's subjects on foot or with Horses and Carriages'. Only the accompanying map declares the true reason for the diversion, showing as it does both the 'present line of park pales' and the 'intended line'.[22]

At one level, of course, the passage of a road through a park was simply aesthetically intrusive. But this was less true of footpaths, and the real objection was not so much to the feature itself as to the people who might use it. As Repton put it in his *Red Book* for Tewin in Hertfordshire:

altho' the late possessor of Tewin Water might think a public road no less appropriate than cheerful immediately in front of the house; or a foot path . . . cutting up the lawn in another direction . . . passing close to the windows, leaving the house on a kind of peninsula surrounded by carts, waggons, gypsies, poachers, &c. &c. who feel they have a right of intrusion. Yet when the place with all its defects shall pass under the correcting hand of good taste, the view from the house will be changed with the views of its possessor.[23]

Making parks

Many writers have emphasized the great sums spent on the creation of landscape parks, often quoting the large amounts of money paid to Capability Brown for those commissions in which he was responsible for the total execution of the design. Certainly, these sums sound a lot, like the £4550 paid by the Third Earl Waldegrave for the changes at Navestock (Essex), or the £5000 spent at nearby Thorndon by Baron Petre.[24] We should, however, remember that these payments were usually spread over several years, and that these were among the wealthiest people in England. In fact, the vast majority of parks seem to have been created quite cheaply.

In 1767, an unknown surveyor prepared a plan of the surroundings of Ditchingham Hall (Norfolk), showing the adjacent fields, the two great avenues leading to the hall, and the walled gardens stretching down to a narrow stream.[25] A marginal text describes the relative heights of various features, the longitudinal gradient of the stream itself, and explains how the map depicts the 'more prominent trees, both in the avenues and on the hills at a distance'. The 'capabilities' of the place were being sized up for improvement, and within a few years the geometric landscape was swept away and replaced by a landscape park. The stream was dammed to form a serpentine lake, while many of the avenue and hedgerow trees were allowed to remain, incorporated into the new landscape as free-standing parkland timber.

All this was standard practice. Many parks contain trees whose girths show that they are older than the park itself, and whose growth pattern indicates that they were once pollarded (Fig. 37). In many cases careful inspection reveals that they stand in lines and on slight banks – the remains of former hedges. Estate accounts reveal that hedgerows were grubbed out and banks levelled when parks were created, but this was seldom done so thoroughly as to leave no archaeological trace. The presence of former hedgerow timber would originally have been more noticeable than it is today, for many of these trees have since died and been replaced. Indeed, many maps made of parks in the nineteenth century show much, sometimes most, of the parkland timber standing in suspiciously straight lines. And most lakes were made like that at Ditchingham, by erecting a small and comparatively inexpensive dam across a valley. Often, little was needed in the way of additional revetment or puddling (lining with clay). Consulting the 'genius of the place' – that is, working with, rather than against, the local landscape and topography – meant, in effect, the creation of an ornamental landscape at comparatively little cost.

37 *North Elmham (Norfolk): pollarded tree, incorporated into the park when it was laid out in the late eighteenth century.*

This is not to deny that a fair amount of money had to be found. The existing gardens needed to be demolished and levelled, and a great deal of new planting took place, particularly on the periphery of the park. Roads often had to be closed, replacements provided, ha-has dug, fences erected. Unfortunately, it is often difficult to use estate archives (even where these survive) to estimate the cost of a park, for the moneys spent on the various activities are usually subsumed under general accounts for estate labour and purchases. In a few cases, however, the owner maintained a separate, itemized account. One example is the 'Various Expenses in the Improvements at Heacham' (Norfolk) between 1768 and 1775, drawn up by Edmund Rolfe.[26] This document provides a fascinating insight into late eighteenth-century park-making.

The entries for the first two years mainly relate to the taking up of field boundaries, the payment of the solicitor for drawing up the writ of *ad quod damnum* for diverting the public road, the laying out of a new road and the erection of oak fences. In the third, fourth, and fifth years there was more levelling and earth-moving, probably for the site of the new house, and trees and more fencing were bought. In 1773 the ha-ha was dug:

Making a sunk fence	£17.0.0
Nails for ditto	£3.17.9
To oak posts, nails and paling for ditto	£32.18.3
Carpenter for ditto	£3.18.6

In the following years, further trees were brought from Mr Aram's nursery in Norwich, and from the park at nearby Houghton, and drives created. When work was completed in 1775, no less than £913 5s 1d had been spent on the park. This may sound like a lot of money. It would certainly have seemed like a lot to Rolfe's gardener, who was paid only £14 per year at the time. But it is not really that much. The work was spread over eight years, during which time Rolfe's annual income seems to have varied between around £1200 and £2300. In other words, in any one year the money expended on the park was between 5 and 10 per cent of his annual income. The sum also needs to be compared with that spent on the kitchen garden, which Rolfe began to construct in 1769. This, we are told in a survey of 1773, covered no more than 1¼ acre, but it cost nearly as much as the entire park to construct and equip – £878 7s 0d (nearly half of which went on the 481,000 bricks used in the walls and greenhouse). In addition, both sums need to be compared with the £4128 1s 4d spent on Rolfe's new house at Heacham, the construction of which began as work on the park and garden was winding down.

In short, the creation of a 'Brownian' park could, and sometimes did, involve a great deal of expense, but it did not have to. A passable version was within the means of all those with serious pretensions to gentility. The park supplied a cheap way of creating an extensive, insulating landscape which was clearly ornamental, but which anyone within the landed classes could afford. It demonstrated land ownership, and elite status, in a highly visible way; and carried with it the resonances of the ancient, 'natural' landscape of the deer park. Yet parks were not only cheap to create. Unlike extensive areas of geometric gardens, which had to be weeded, mowed and clipped, parks were cheap to maintain. The open turf had to be grazed, but money could be made from this, and also from the commercial

exploitation of the woods and plantations within, and around, the park. The landowner could, as it were, have his cake and eat it. The landscape park was the ideal solution to the quest for 'affordable magnificence' which had been begun by Tory writers in the early decades of the century.

Challenges to the Brownian park

The open, naturalistic park did not triumph easily over earlier, geometric concepts of landscape design. Owners were often reluctant to rip up avenues, and fell geometric plantations, which were only just coming to maturity. Many landscapes were, in fact, 'deformalized' through decay and neglect, and only took on a truly 'Brownian' appearance in the early years of the nineteenth century. Moreover, the park only gradually supplanted the garden as the principal setting for the house, and never entirely. Many members of the provincial gentry clung on to their enclosed courts, lawns and fruit trees until the very end of the eighteenth century. Even when their walled enclosures were finally demolished, many of the aesthetic aspects of the old gardens migrated to the still-walled kitchen garden. And contrary to popular belief, shrubberies and pleasure grounds evolved rather than disappeared completely in this period. Even Brown continued, throughout his career, to include within many of his designs an area of mown grass, gravelled paths, shrubs and flowers to one side of the principal elevation of the house: pleasure grounds less elaborate than those of the 1740s and 1750s, but pleasure grounds nevertheless. Thus at Youngesbury (Hertfordshire), the area to the south-east of the house is marked on Brown's plan as 'Pleasure Ground', and the indigenous trees which dominated the rest of the design were here accompanied by shrubs and various conifers.[27]

Yet while such features survived, they were now marginalized or hidden, so as not to detract from the isolation of the house, and this rejection of detail and intimacy caused some disquiet among writers on garden design. In 1762, Lord Kames advocated the establishment of 'theme gardens' near the house, an idea reiterated ten years later by William Chambers, whose *Dissertation on Oriental Gardens* urged that gardens with complex and varied planting should be a prominent part of the country house landscape.[28] Some did more than just write, even at the height of Brown's popularity and influence. In 1781, William Emes placed a circular flower garden immediately below the windows of the new drawing room at Sandon (Staffordshire).[29]

The even, open appearance of the park itself also had its critics. Chambers castigated it as bland and dull, and William Gilpin compared its stereotyped, smooth beauty unfavourably with 'picturesque' beauty, a more varied concept, involving roughness of texture and ruggedness.[30] Gilpin's ideas were further developed by Richard Payne Knight and Uvedale Price in their respective publications of 1794, *The Landscape* and *Essays on the Picturesque*.[31] These men argued that landscapes should have variety, and should attempt to capture the form and spirit of paintings by artists like Salvator Rosa, and emphasize the drama of the wilder scenes of nature, rather than the muted pastoral of Brown. Cliffs, cascades, wild wooded hillsides and winding paths, and thicker, wilder planting were not, however, to everyone's taste, nor, indeed, possible in most places, due to the nature of the local terrain.[32] In the highland zone, at places like Knight's own home at Downton (Hereford and Worcester), the geology might provide suitable raw material for organizing landscapes along these somewhat crazy lines. Elsewhere, 'picturesque' notions had a more subtle impact on the landscape. In many places, a veneer of more varied, wilder and irregular planting was added to the smoothness of the Brownian park, as at Cassiobury (Hertfordshire), where Knight himself probably advised on the planting. By 1837:

Immediately beyond the lawn, to the east, is a part of the park, abounding with large and grand forest-trees, interspersed with furze, thorn &c., forming a striking contrast to the dressed scenes adjoining the house.[33]

By this time, the park and the surrounding estate land here had been provided with a number of suitably picturesque buildings, in a variety of primitive and rustic styles (Fig. 38).

In many places, tree clumps were made to appear more irregular and romantic by underplanting with hawthorn or holly. Often, several trees and bushes were planted in a single hole, to ensure a denser and wilder pattern of growth. Pine trees, and especially the Scots pine, were sometimes planted within the parkland, again because of their irregular, romantic form. Such touches seem in some places to have gone hand in hand with changes in the pattern of land-use within the park. It was grazed less intensively, in order to allow low-growing shrubs and bushes to establish themselves, and to provide a rougher growth of grass, rather different from the close-cropped turf of most eighteenth-century parks.

Such techniques do not seem to have been adopted on a very wide scale, however, and were less important than the more general reorganization of the layout of landscapes advocated by picturesque designers. Because the view from the house should appear as a picture, it had to have a frame – a foreground – as well as a middle ground and a distance. A foreground was lacking in Brown's sweeping parkland, so in the early years of the nineteenth century picturesque designers like William Sawrey Gilpin (William Gilpin's nephew) reinstated terraces, shrubberies and even parterres in

38 *Keeper's Lodge, Cassiobury Park, Watford (Hertfordshire): from John Britton's* History and Description of Cassiobury Park. *This, and other elaborate buildings in and around the park, may have been designed by Sir Jeffry Wyatville.*

front of the main facade. Brown's parks, moreover, had no distant views because of the encircling belt. Picturesque designers broke this at intervals, allowing in selected, distant glimpses of the local countryside.

The view from the house was not the only thing that concerned the picturesque theorists and designers, however. They were also keen to create landscapes which contained features and details which had to be discovered, through exploration, and their designs made far greater use of paths than those of Brown. These took the walker past various ornamental features and

buildings – often in a gothic or 'rustic' style – which did not form part of the main view from the house, but which revealed themselves gradually, as the walker turned a bend in the path, or caught sight of them a little distance away, half-hidden in the undergrowth.

It was, however, Humphry Repton who mounted the most effective challenge to the Brownian park. Born in 1752, he pursued a series of largely unsuccessful careers before launching out, in 1788, as a 'landscape gardener'.[34] What he lacked in previous experience he made up for with useful social contacts. He had been personal assistant to William Wyndham, Chief Secretary to the Lord Lieutenant of Ireland and a well-connected politician. Repton liked to think of himself as Brown's successor, and his treatment of the park did, to a large extent, mirror that of Brown. But his landscapes, like those of the contemporary picturesque designers, tended to be more heavily planted, livelier and more intimately considered. And, again like the proponents of the picturesque, Repton placed more emphasis on the pleasure-ground and shrubbery, allowing them to intrude more and more into the landscape. By 1799, he was placing a terrace between the house and the park, and in the early 1800s, working in conjunction with his son, Repton increasingly introduced formal gardens, even parterres, in front of the main facade.

Repton thus had more in common with the picturesque designers than their often acrimonious disagreements would suggest. Indeed, to all intents and purposes he was one of them. Like them, he thought in terms of pictures, something clear from his *Red Books*, beautifully illustrated design proposals which he prepared for many of his clients. These included clever 'before and after' views with a lift-off flap. Not only his treatment of the park and the foreground, but also that of the more distant view, had much in common with the ideas of Knight and Price. He, too, reacted against the excessively enclosed nature of the eighteenth-century park, and advocated the breaking of the belt at intervals in order to allow glimpses of the more acceptable aspects of the countryside beyond. He liked the suggestion of human presence, indicated by the curving spiral of smoke above the trees from a distant cottage chimney.

Where he differed from the picturesque school was in his insistence that the landscape should not only be seen, but used: the grounds of a country house were more than a picture, they were a setting for a

range of activities, and must combine 'beauty and utility'. Hence his preference for a smooth greensward, rather than the rougher ground beloved of Price and Knight, for parks had to be heavily grazed, if they were to be an economic proposition for most landowners.

Both Repton, and the leading prophets of the picturesque, saw landscape design as an activity with social, even political, implications. The philosophy of Price and Knight was complex and at times contradictory, seeing the freedom of nature – as expressed in wild landscapes – as intimately connected with the freedom of the individual. Repton's ideas were more straightforward, and more in keeping with the times. To him, the Brownian park symbolized the exclusivity of the landed elite, their rejection of a paternalistic involvement in the life of the local community. This exclusivity, as the French revolution erupted on the other side of the channel, he considered increasingly foolhardy, and dangerous.[35] To Repton, then, the breaks in the perimeter belt expressed the connection between the landowner and the local community. Similarly, the extension of landscaping beyond the boundaries of the park (something he termed 'appropriation') would also serve to show the involvement of the owner in the life of the wider countryside, as well as emphasizing his importance:

The first essential of greatness in a place is the appearance of united and uninterrupted property.[36]

Repton often advocated planting up the public road as an avenue, and in 1790 he suggested that the same kind of white paling should be used everywhere on the Livermere estate (Suffolk), including the nearby village.

Repton was no radical. A paternalistic Tory, he had an almost mystical faith in the ancient landed families of England. Paradoxically, he rarely did more than add a few details to their parks, which had already, for the most part, been landscaped by Brown. It was a source of constant grief that many of his clients were the parvenu merchants and industrialists who – as always – benefited from wartime conditions. For there was much about Repton's style that made it eminently suitable for the grounds of those whose carriage drive was relatively short – for the smaller parks proliferating in the landscape at the turn of the nineteenth century. Moreover, his copious publications allowed his ideas to be widely copied. Much of his style was, in fact, about illusion: about making estates appear larger and more important than they really were. His treatment of entrances was widely emulated. Brown had provided his clients with imposing drives which left the public road at right angles, and then meandered around the edge of the park, providing ample views of its vast size. Repton's drives were more direct, and planted in such a way that only selected glimpses of the park were usually allowed, thus enabling its true size to be obscured. His drives left the road, not with an abrupt turn, but in a smooth curve. Otherwise, as he said of Honing (Norfolk), the road would seem 'to lead to some other place of greater importance beyond it'.

His emphasis on gardens and pleasure grounds – an emphasis shared by picturesque designers of the early nineteenth century like Gilpin – struck a chord with a wider social group, those who could never afford a park, even a small one, the middle classes whose economic, social and eventually political importance was increasing in the first half of the nineteenth century. And it was to this group, rather than to the country landowners alone, that professional designers and writers increasingly turned their attention in the years after Repton's death in 1816.

5 The nineteenth century

The nineteenth century saw Britain emerge as the most economically powerful nation in the world: the first country to experience an industrial revolution, and the ruler of a vast empire. Cities expanded dramatically and a manufacturing and professional middle class grew in numbers and in wealth. There was a massive increase, not only in the scale of production, but also in the scale of consumption, which made the 'consumer revolution' of the previous century seem like small beer. All these profound changes had, in one way or another, an effect on garden design. And it was *gardens*, rather than parks, which were the key feature of the nineteenth century. The return of the garden to its position in front of the main facade of the house, pioneered by Repton and others at the start of the century, was never reversed; gardens grew steadily in variety, scale and sophistication.

There were two main reasons for this. Partly, the popularity of gardens was related to fashions in architecture. In this rapidly changing world, there was an increasing enthusiasm for houses designed in a broadly Gothic or Jacobean style, symbolic of an older, supposedly more stable and harmonious age. Other alternatives to the classical Palladian of the eighteenth century were also freely experimented with in this eclectic age, especially a form of Italianate Renaissance architecture. Country houses built in these styles looked best standing, not isolated in open parkland, but beside gardens, especially gardens of a geometric nature. These provided a transition from the formal, architectural structure of the building to the informal, 'natural' environment of the park.

The popularity of the garden was also related to the increasing economic and cultural importance of the middle classes, who provided an ever-increasing market for horticultural goods, technology and services – a veritable 'consumer revolution' in gardening. This was not an entirely new development, for nurseries, in particular, had been growing in numbers and size during the previous century; their growth now continued and a range of other services proliferated. In particular, in the nineteenth century more people benefited from the skills of landscape designers than ever before. Not only did landscape gardeners work for a much wider social group, their influence now extended through their writings and through their designs for public open spaces. Loudon, Nesfield and Paxton were probably the best known and most influential designers of this period.

John Claudius Loudon was born in 1783, the son of a Lanarkshire farmer. By the time he moved to London at the age of 20 he was an accomplished draughtsman and had served an apprenticeship with an Edinburgh nursery. The aim of his move south was to establish himself as a landscape gardener. In his first book, published the following year, he stated 'I believe that I am the first who has set out as a landscape gardener, professing to follow Mr Price's principles',[1] and his success in so doing can be seen in the landscape he created around the now ruined Barnbarroch, near Wigton (Cumbria). But he was highly adaptable, and in areas like East Anglia, which had rather less scope for this kind of picturesque landscaping, his designs were more closely allied to those of Repton. His work at Gillingham (Norfolk) (1812) reveals a further degree of flexibility.[2] Here he proposed two alternative designs: the 'ancient' and the 'modern'. The 'modern' was a version of the landscape park, but the 'ancient' included an avenue approach, and Reptonesque 'appropriation' of the adjoining fields and public roads through judicious planting. This was a scheme calculated to provide a fitting setting for the ancient mansion of Gillingham Hall. Loudon's versatility, and willingness to adapt his ideas to suit individual client's tastes, ultimately denied him identity as a designer of the wider landscape. It was chiefly in his ideas for the grounds nearer the house that he was to make his major contribution.

If the eighteenth century can be defined as the search for nature, the nineteenth can be said to be the century in which the myth that man could successfully imitate nature was dispelled. Loudon's view was simple: by all means admire nature but acknowledge that the art of gardening is the art of changing it. Such an art should be recognizable and conspicuous in order to be fully appreciated. His theories became embodied in a style known as 'Gardenesque', because it was particularly appropriate for gardens and pleasure grounds. The shift in emphasis fitted in well with the keen interest in the wave of new exotics which swept the country in the nineteenth century, a notable side-effect (and, indeed, symbol) of imperial power. Plants were no longer to be viewed only as part of a wider picture or design; they were to stand out as individual

specimens. This did not mean that single specimens should stand isolated, but that each should be identifiable within a group by a clear-cut distinction from its neighbour in colour, form or texture.

Perhaps Loudon's greatest direct impact on the landscape was through the design of cemeteries and public parks (he even produced a plan for green belts around London).[3] But it was not his practice as a designer which enabled his ideas to be disseminated so widely, it was the scale of his literary output. He published over thirty books, many of which ran to several editions, and wrote extensively for periodicals and magazines, some of which he was instrumental in establishing. Like so many other gardeners in the century, Loudon did not simply confine himself to horticulture and landscape design, but wrote extensively on agriculture and architecture. His confidence in the importance of his opinions enabled him to embrace such topics as etiquette, the hiring of servants and the best way to keep rabbits.[4]

Like Repton, William Andrews Nesfield had no gardening background and came to landscape gardening through painting. The son of the rector of Brancepath (Durham), Nesfield trained as an engineer at Woolwich, serving with the army until he was 23, when he retired on half-pay in order to paint. His entry into the profession of landscape design may have been under the auspices of his brother-in law, the architect Anthony Salvin. He was certainly heavily influenced by the architects with whom he worked, as well as by the formal gardens of previous centuries. From the 1840s Nesfield had an extensive practice. His own grounds, around his house at Muswell Hill, displayed a refined transition between the garden and the wider landscape with a simple parterre, borrowed landscape views and sheep grazing in his small pasture.[5] But his professional work was flamboyant and sometimes controversial. He is perhaps best known for his elaborate parterres, for which he was greatly in demand. His commissions included Holkham (Norfolk), Stoke Edith (Herefordshire), Arundel Castle (Sussex), Alnwick (Northumberland) and, perhaps his most magnificent, Witley Court in Worcestershire where his design formed part of the first Earl of Dudley's quarter of a million pound aggrandizement schemes.[6]

Initially, Nesfield's parterres were based on those from seventeenth- and early eighteenth-century gardening texts, or on early maps or plans of the places at which he worked. Thus at Worsley Hall (Lancashire) he used one of Dezallier d'Argenville's designs and at Drayton (Northamptonshire) and Stoke Edith (Herefordshire) he restored the gardens to their form prior to 'landscaping'. From the 1850s, however, he became increasingly interested in the Tudor period, for which few actual plans survive, and he experimented freely with coloured gravels and with the laying out of family arms and monograms.

His work was ideally suited to the Italianate schemes of architect colleagues, and he worked closely, in particular, with Robert Burn and Sir Charles Barry. The greatest scheme resulting from the latter partnership was undoubtedly the garden of Shrublands (Suffolk), which still survives in recognizable condition. Nesfield was also responsible for some of the landscaping at Kew and for the gardens of the Royal Horticultural Society at Kensington (although these were much criticized for the predominance of non-horticultural elements). From 1871 Nesfield was joined in his partnership by his sons, Markham and William Eden Nesfield. Markham designed the Italian garden at Regent's Park; William Eden achieved a measure of fame as an architect and surrounded some of his houses with gardens based on his father's designs.[7]

Joseph Paxton was probably the most versatile and energetic of the nineteenth-century designers. Born the son of a Bedfordshire farmer, at 15 he went to be garden boy at Battlesden, near Woburn (Bedfordshire). He spent a short period employed at Woodhall (Hertfordshire), before returning to Battlesden where, at the age of 19, he was responsible for a major landscape construction in the form of a new lake. Shortly afterwards he moved to the Duke of Somerset's home at Wimbledon, and from there to the newly-opened gardens of the Horticultural Society at Chiswick. His skill must have been evident since he was approached by the Duke of Devonshire (later president of the society) to become head gardener at Chatsworth (Derbyshire) – no small position for a man of 23. Here he transformed the gardens, making major new waterworks and planting the arboretum. His horticultural skill and enthusiasm were unparalleled. He persuaded the Duke to send plant hunting expeditions abroad, he was awarded numerous medals from the Horticultural Society, and it was he who first coaxed the *Victoria Regia* to flower in this country – in a glasshouse designed to his own specification. Paxton, who was as much an engineer and architect as a gardener, perfected a system of ridge-and-furrow roofing for glass buildings which was an important technical advance; designed the Great Stove at Chatsworth; and went on to create the Crystal Palace at Sydenham, complete with its landscaped grounds (Fig. 39). Indeed, the majority of his designs were for public open spaces; his activities in the private sphere were largely limited to the Duke of Devonshire's estates. Designs like Chatsworth or Sydenham included formal gardens whose layout expressed Paxton's confidence in his wealth of acquired horticultural and technical skills.

Not as prolific a writer as Loudon, Paxton was neverthless the author of several works and was instrumental in founding botanical magazines. As well as being a designer and technical innovator, Paxton became a railway company director, wealthy property

39 *The Crystal Palace, Sydenham, c.1890.*

owner and Member of Parliament. He was knighted in 1851. There can have been few people in Britain at the end of his life who were unaware of Sir Joseph Paxton.[8]

Loudon, Nesfield and Paxton are still famous. But there were other prolific designers and writers in this period. Two were trained by Paxton at Chatsworth. Edward Kemp (1817–91) was responsible for a number of public parks, cemeteries and private commissions, as well as being author of *How to Lay Out a Small Garden*. Edward Milner (1819–84) also worked on public parks but he is best remembered as a designer for millionaire industrialists at such sites as Bodnant and Highbury.

Yet as in previous centuries, well-known professional designers like these accounted for only a very small proportion of gardens and landscapes. Others were created by

architects, who were increasingly involved in the design of gardens as part of the overall design of the house. And, as in the eighteenth century, there were numerous 'minor' designers, men like Mr Malcolm, of Stockwell Place in Middlesex, who styled himself 'Land Surveyor' and put the following advertisement in the Norfolk Chronicle in 1800:

Mr Malcolm most respectfully offers his services to those noblemen and gentlemen who, for ornament or profit, are disposed to make alteration in their grounds, gardens and parks this season. He begs to submit various designs in Pleasure Ground, Park and Forest scenery, decorative and other buildings, water etc.[9]

Mr Malcolm was one of many designers who never made the history books but whose practice, as can be seen from the advertisement, was considerably more than a local enterprise. Simpler offers in the press of 'designs and plans prepared'[10] provided a cheaper option. Loudon disapproved vehemently of these enterprises.

Nothing can display a greater want of judgement than the practice of those gentlemen who get only a general plan from a professional person and then send for a nurseryman to fill up the plantations or shrubberies with trees.[11]

Many designs were made by the nurserymen themselves, and this again was a practice of which Loudon disapproved, but not a new one in the nineteenth century. And who better to know what plants would flourish best in difficult situations? Moreover, the employment of a nursery to produce and carry through a design meant an owner could dispense with the potentially fraught, and frequently expensive, practice of sub-contracting. The diversity of the work nurserymen were prepared to undertake in this period can be seen in the advertisement for Benjamin Samuel Williams, of the Victoria and Paradise Nurseries in Upper Holloway, in 1876:

Landscape and sub-tropical gardening. Estimates, Plans and advice given for the laying out of Parks, Pleasure grounds, Rockwork, Ferneries etc.

as well as 'erecting greenhouses and conservatories'.[12]

As in the previous century, many men and women also designed their own gardens, taking advantage of the vast number of manuals produced by Loudon and his less gifted contemporaries. If the efforts of Lady Lothian at Blickling were

40 *The east parterre, Blickling (Norfolk), c.1895. Designed by the owner, Lady Lothian.*

representative, however, the results may not always have been what the authors intended (Fig. 40).

The increase in the number of designers, and in the range of books and magazines devoted to gardening, was one symptom of the intensifying pace of consumerism in nineteenth-century society. Another was the proliferation of 'technical consumables' – fixtures, devices and gadgets. Indeed, it is impossible to study landscape and garden design in the nineteenth century without recognizing the enormous influence of a rapidly developing technology, allied with an expanding communications network. Improvements in the manufacture of glass and cast iron were responsible both for the widespread distribution of ornamental glasshouses, and for the means to heat and service them. The conservatory and the covered 'conservative' wall were products of the same technology. Garden equipment was improved and time-saving devices such as wheeled water-sprinklers (initially developed to cut down dust on railway stations) were mass-produced. Budding's lawnmower, invented in the early 1830s (although not marketed immediately), radically altered the appearance of lawns, and reduced the time taken to cut them. It may well have been responsible for the proliferation of this feature in small gardens.

The Wardian Case, which enabled whole plants to survive the long sea journeys from their homeland to Britain, proved a major advance in the importation of exotics. And shipping itself was now in general faster and safer, so that new discoveries could be transported more easily. Once home, better glasshouses with reliable heating and watering systems ensured that propagation had the maximum chance of success. And when propagated the plants could be widely advertised for sale, and distributed with ease on improved road and new rail networks.

As the nineteenth century progressed, so too did the multi-dimensional spiral of horticultural consumerism. Thus, for example, the more plants which were introduced, the more nurseries were able to specialize; the more species were brought together, the more varieties could be propagated. With enough varieties the species became collectable which in turn increased demand. Improved communications brought wider distribution; nurseries could no longer rely on local custom and survived by specializing, which they were able to do because of the increase in new plants and greater demand.

Visits to botanical gardens, subscription to *Curtis's Magazine of Botany* (or any one of a range of similar publications) and membership of the local horticultural society, were all part of everyday life for the Victorian garden owner. The search for horticultural novelty, and the desire to startle neighbours and friends with ever more exotic specimens blossoming in the conservatory, was a national obsession even before the Great Exhibition. And if one could point out plants collected at one's own instigation, or new varieties, propagated on the premises and bearing one's own name, prestige was readily accorded. The fact that so many of these varieties were not commercially propagated has obscured just how many people delighted in producing them. A glance at the Transactions and later publications of the Horticultural Society will serve to emphasize not only how many plants have been lost but how many we might not recognize if transported back to the nineteenth-century garden.

The road from town

Rising populations and the intensification of industry made towns and cities increasingly unpopular places to live. Selected spas and seaside towns might have their share of fashionable clientele, but the socially ambitious distanced their residences as far and as fast as possible from the centres of commerce: the length of the road from town was a measure of status and success. At one end were the landed magnates of Blenheim, Chatsworth and Holkham, at the other was the industrial worker in his terraced house. As industrialization gathered pace, the countryside was progressively invested with mythical qualities of peace and simplicity, notions which still distort our perception of rural life.

If Edward Kemp and other writers are to be believed, the lowest form of horticultural dabbling was in the centre of the capital city: the cockney garden.[13] As the pariah of landscape design, individual gardens were not documented in the same way as more acceptable styles, although mirror globes, to reflect the plant colours,[14] and rockworks formed in shells were cited as examples of the vulgarity of their features. Class-consciousness presumably explains why these things were anathema to a generation which happily connived at the family arms or monograms laid out in bedding plants[15] or parrots on poles selected so that the plumage matched the plants.[16]

The villa in the suburbs was at least one, and, depending upon whether the town in question was Bath or Birmingham and the house detached or semi-detached, sometimes several, rungs up the social ladder. Its garden was of limited size, ranging from around half an acre to a maximum of about three (Fig. 41). Of all nineteenth-century gardens that of the suburban villa probably suffered most from standardization of design. The style of edging tiles, the pattern and colour of annuals in the 'best' border, or the specimens for shrubbery or conservatory, often appeared to offer an endless selection, but it was choice within a rigid framework. Size was one limiting factor, the opinion of the neighbours was another since there was, from at least the mid-century, a definite

accepted model for suburban garden design: a well-manicured lawn with trim beds of varying shapes and patterns; a shrubbery with single specimen trees (evergreen shrubs such as *Euonymus* predominated for obvious reasons); Monkey Puzzles joined such specimen exotics as yuccas on the front lawn; a lean-to conservatory flanked the house and collections of chrysanthemums, dahlias and roses ornamented special areas of the garden. A separate fruit and vegetable area was situated to the rear of the house, at the 'bottom' of the garden.

Where a park had belts for exclusion, the suburban garden had a shrubbery, a statement of exclusivity, and a symbolic protection against real or imagined intrusion.

Every beautiful flower that unfolds itself, or shrub that spreads out its attractive berries about Christmas time, affords so many temptations to pilfering for the passers-by . . . who will be unable to resist the inducement.[17]

Paxton went as far as to suggest that gentlemen in towns would be better subscribing to a walled, communal vegetable garden, that could be locked, than attempting to grow produce in the gardens around their own homes.[18]

Further out of town, and preferably separated from it by at least a notional 'green belt', small-scale industrialists and professionals bought up plots according to their means, and built and developed.

. . . To live amidst fields and gardens, and cultivated or unassisted nature, or to have only the vicinity of kindred or superior places, is a luxury well worth the sacrifice of some trifling convenience and the travelling of a mile or two further from town.[19]

Their grounds had more in common with the towns they had just left than with the countryside. They might, for decorative reasons, have sheep grazing on the minute 'parkland' known as 'The Lawn' or include a

41 *Suburban villa gardens on the outskirts of Cambridge, as shown on the Ordnance Survey, 25" to the mile map of 1886.*

small arable field as an incident in a walk, but most would have followed the principles of the owner described by Augustus Jessop:

. . . he goes in for fancy breeds and runs up an ornamental 'walk' for them, he likes to look at them . . . He keeps a gardener too, and exhibits his roses against the country. 'Sell my vegetables'

said one of them to me with some warmth. 'I'm not brought to that yet. Do you take me for a nurseryman?'[20]

Business was exactly what they were trying to leave behind. However, many of these gardens were, and some still are, a refreshing expression of new-found independence. Cragg Wood, between Apperley Bridge and Rawdon (in Yorkshire), is today a wilderness dotted with the decaying remains of the mansions and garden buildings built by Bradford's Victorian merchants. The first to arrive was Robert Milligan, a Scot from an Ayrshire family, who made his fortune wholesaling cloth. By 1831 he was ready to move out of town, and chose the Cragg Wood site, less than 8km (5 miles) from his city warehouse. He bought up 80ha (200 acres) of the Layton estate, and was soon followed by his partner, Nathaniel Briggs, who was instrumental in laying out a series of building plots, covenanted to be not less than 3ha (7 acres). Water-meadows by the Aire and a section of the wood itself (improved by grottoes, rockwork and stairways), were left as 'natural' features. As well as containing private residences, this was to be home to institutions of varying nature, and the first president of the Yorkshire Baptist Training College waxed lyrical over the picturesque site:

. . . We are clasped in nature's arms, surrounded by wooded depths, green winding walks, moss grown rocks bracken clothed, where anemones and hyacinths find the home they love.

The names of the houses were as splendid and varied as their gardens: Acacia; Buckstone Hall; Woodleigh; and one can only guess at the exotic nature of the garden of 'Zimbabwe', the weekend villa of the founder of Mansell and Hatchers Orchid Nursery. Privacy was a major concern of these refugee members of the middle class. At Cragg Wood the name of 'Spite and Malice Ginnel' records the animosity between neighbouring owners whose grounds this path separated.[21]

Indeed at this social level, as at others, enormous efforts were usually made to ensure seclusion. Heavy belts of trees and shrubs were planted on boundaries, and owners tried hard to reduce the impact of roads and footpaths. In 1855 Edward Kemp laid out the grounds around a rectory in Worcestershire, on land purchased the previous year. A public footpath led from the road to the church, across the proposed pleasure grounds. The rector's desire for privacy obviously overcame his desire to view the congregation going to church. The path was sunk and a bank thrown up against the pleasure ground. Kemp assured him that by '. . . covering the bank with evergreen shrubs, it will soon cease to intrude itself on the more private grounds'.[22]

Still within travelling distance of the city or market town, on which they depended for their livelihoods, some professionals and industrialists bought up larger tracts of land. Their houses overlooked the small parks they created, separated by a mandatory single terrace, with low planting and a shrubbery or cluster of exotic trees to one side. They laid out informal woodland walks, modest formal gardens with a range of ornamental glass, and they farmed adjoining land in a rather half-hearted fashion. These people had little experience of farming, nor, in most cases, any desire or need to manage an estate economically. The small farm, the standard layout and the heavy use of 'borrowed' landscape are indicative both of the limited scale of these establishments and of the absence of economic involvement in the countryside.

Underscar, near Keswick (Cumbria), is a good example. William Oxley, the owner, took full advantage of a steeply sloping site (a fall of over 46m (150ft) from house to boundary), adjoining the 'woods and park-like fields of Ormthwaite Hall'. A stream ran through the site and along the southern boundary. The carriage-drive wound through the 'field' approaching the house. This was not long enough to warrant a lodge, although Oxley had been keen to have one. To the south-east of the house was a small terraced formal garden, regularly laid out and approached from either house

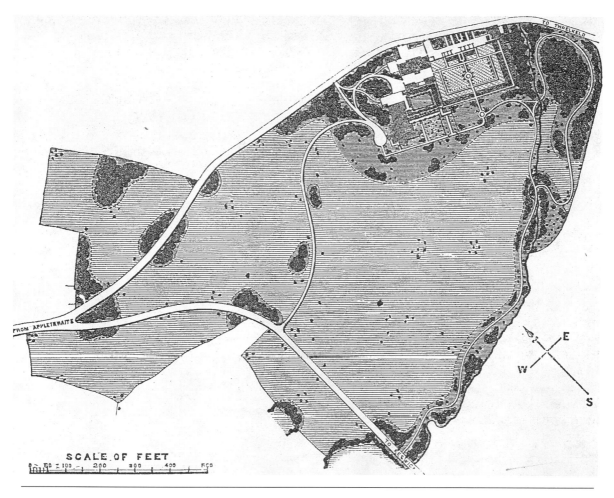

42   *Plan of Underscar, Keswick (Cumbria), by Edward Kemp, c.1860.*

or conservatory. To the north-east lay the kitchen garden, reached via the formal garden but out of sight of the main house. Below the terrace a serpentine open fence separated an area planted informally with shrubs from the main area of park. The pleasure ground or shrubbery extended in picturesque fashion along the banks of the stream (Fig. 42). Mr Oxley had acquired, in addition to the block of land between the roads, several small portions of land on the other side of them.

The planting is so contrived as to assist in uniting the outside fields with the principle enclosure, and the fences (which are hedges) are kept low in order to aid this object.[23]

The spread of towns and cities, in the present century, has enveloped many of these landscapes. A few have been used for public parks, more have been divided and built over and still more have fallen victim to the ever-increasing road network. The views out from the grounds, on which many of these designs heavily depended, have often been changed out of recognition. The best survivals are, understandably, around towns with a well-preserved rural hinterland (Underscar is still largely intact).

More usually, examples of such nineteenth-century landscapes survive as islands in a sea of encroaching urbanization.

The established landscape

Not all small designs like these were the creations of the refugee businessman. Minor members of the established rural gentry, and the more prosperous members of the clergy, created similar layouts deep in the countryside. For, in spite of the increasing numbers of people who wished to live 'amidst fields and gardens', rural areas in the nineteenth century continued to be dominated by the landed gentry and aristocracy. Even when the real source of their wealth lay elsewhere – for there were many established landowners who made fortunes from exploiting mineral resources beneath their estates, or from urban developments – country life remained central to the existence of such people. Successful financiers and industrialists bought up, or leased, country estates and adopted the same self-consciously rural lifestyle. Building on the advice first offered by Repton, this now involved adopting the role of benevolent landlord, and the kind of landscape that went with it. Increasingly, this was intended to assuage criticism of rural living conditions, and aristocratic privilege, from an increasingly vocal, and essentially urban, middle class. In 1816 Repton wrote:

Let us restore that sort of importance which formerly belonged to the old Manor House; where the proprietor resided among his tenants, not only to collect the rents, but to share the produce of his estate with his humble dependants; and where plenteous hospitality was not sacrificed to the ostentatious refinements of luxury.[24]

But such an idealistic vision could never have been realized, because it failed to take into account inherent social conflicts. On the one hand owners wanted to forge more harmonious class relations; on the other they were keen to maintain the division between themselves and their social inferiors, and retain privacy. In practice, only parts of Repton's programme for maintaining a 'happy medium betwixt Licentious Equality and Oppressive Tyranny' were ever widely adopted.[25]

Landowners held tenants dinners and dances in the park to celebrate the coming of age of an heir, or the election of the owner to parliament. Interestingly there seems to have been a tendency, as the century progressed, for such gatherings to become more formal and for them to be held on the terrace where the close proximity to the 'big house' had, if the pictures are anything to go by, a sobering effect. Village sports, too, crossed park and social boundaries. A small area for a cricket ground could easily be afforded out of the acres of parkland, and estate workers were encouraged to hold matches in which the owner and his family participated. Small lakes and ponds could be used for skating in the winter and some owners constructed special skating rinks. The finer points of benevolence, however, seem to have escaped the Duke of Portland, who made skating on the rink at Welbeck (Nottinghamshire) compulsory for staff.[26]

Estate housing came in for rigorous examination and extensive improvement. Earlier 'model villages', like Houghton (Norfolk), had largely been constructed for practical reasons, to replace settlements destroyed by emparking. In the nineteenth century, however, estate villages also enhanced an owner's prestige by demonstrating his care for the estate community. But, just as it was the landowner's initials which were seen on estate houses, so it was his hand which was to be seen in the front gardens. The back garden could be devoted to the pig and the vegetables; the front was visible, and not to be left to the tender mercies of the uneducated tenant (perhaps owners feared the country equivalent of the cockney garden). Thus, in the early 1860s, Edward Kemp remodelled the village just outside the park gates at Daylesford (Gloucestershire) for Harmon Grisewood:

All the front gardens are laid out in one area, with as few walks crossing it as possible and groups of evergreen and deciduous shrubs scattered sparingly about. These front gardens are to be maintained in order by Mr Grisewood and not by the individual cottagers.[27]

In his picturesque village at Harlaxton (Lincolnshire), Gregory Gregory went as far as to specify which climbing plants were to grow up each house wall.[28] Box hedges still define walks in many of these cottage gardens and are reminiscent of a time when

the neat estate cottages around a village green, the church, the estate school and the regular cricket matches and tenants feasts symbolized an ordered and apparently contented estate community (Fig. 43). But at the head was the patriarchal landlord who, having settled the rural workers, could withdraw into his house and park.

This conflict between the desire for separation and the need for openness was delicately handled by Kemp at Daylesford

. . . A plantation shutting in the whole [of the village] from the park but so arranged that at intervals, beautiful glimpses of the park are obtained, between the cottages, from the village road.[29]

This was typical: the parkland belts were only broken at intervals, in order to allow in selected, suitably 'picturesque' views.

43   *One of a series of estate village gardens, Catton (Norfolk). Each garden had a different pattern of box hedging and was the responsibility of estate gardeners.*

Indeed, in most parts of the country the landscape park seems to have become *more* hemmed in by belts as the nineteenth century progressed. In 1834 Talleyrand's niece, the Duchess de Dino observed:

English people . . . hate to be seen, and to secure privacy, are quite willing to dispense with an extended view . . . You need not hope to amuse yourself by watching the movements of the passers-by, the travellers, the peasants working in the fields, the villages or the surrounding country. Green lawns, the flowers round about the house, and splendid trees which block all vistas – these are what they love and what you find almost everywhere.[30]

There was also a marked increase in the number of gate lodges built throughout the period. In 1710 it would have been rare to find a park-gate lodge anywhere. Although by 1780 most great landowners had a keeper installed at the gate, it was not until the following century that most members of the local gentry found the need for such measures. By 1880 there were few residences of any importance without lodges, although these served to do more than merely deter intruders. As Repton had been keenly aware, the strategic placing of a lodge could considerably extend the apparent boundaries of an otherwise small park, and serve to signal the presence of a country house to passers-by.

Park-making schemes, as in the previous century, had an effect on the local communications network. But it was now more difficult to close public roads and footpaths, due to the vocal opposition from middle-class residents. Landowners had to

44 *Embankment on the north side of the park, Avishayes (Somerset).*

45 *Lithograph of the Leeds and Selby railway by R. Martin, c.1830. Note the heavy planting shielding Mr Walker's park from the line of the railway.*

find other ways of dealing with the intrusion they presented. The level of roads was sometimes lowered: sunken roads or footpaths were invisible from a house on an eminence, and the parkland landscape on both sides therefore appeared continuous. At Shendish (Hertfordshire) the public path was first rerouted further from the house, and then sunk 1.5m (5ft) below ground level, with a wall erected on either side to prevent people scaling the banks. Where the footpath crossed the main drive, it was sunk even further beneath a 'viaduct', deep enough to allow the passage of a cart.[31] Major roads were more of a problem and sometimes expensive measures were taken to minimize their impact. Avishayes, near Chard (Somerset), had a public road curving around the northern boundary of the park. At some time in the early nineteenth century the boundary here was raised in a great bank, nearly 1½m (4ft) high, with trees closely planted along the top. This still forms a prominent feature in the landscape (Fig. 44).

Those with the greatest power and influence, however, could still have roads diverted. They could also influence the line of the new railways. At first sight, it might seem that early railways posed less of a threat to the landscape than roads. Trains were less frequent than road traffic, and there was no danger of trespass or of travellers lingering. But the relative straightness of the route, together with the massive schemes of earth-moving involved, which uncovered vast stretches of bare soil, meant that railways were regarded in a similar way to today's motorways (Fig. 45). The opposition of the fifth Duke of Portland to the railways running outside his park at Welbeck in 1864 shows a further similarity. The Duke argued that the pollution emanating from locomotives would damage the ancient oaks of Sherwood forest embedded in his estate woodland, about 2km (1¼ miles) from the proposed line, and nearly 8km (5 miles) from Welbeck. One of the Duke of Portland's agents summed up the landowners' fear of railway companies: '. . . if all their schemes were carried out they would cut up Notts into pie meat'.[32] The real objection of rural landowners, however, was to pollution of a more human nature, for the railways represented the pernicious influence of industry, of the manufacturing towns, spreading like tentacles through the countryside. There was an element of double-think here. The 'not in my back yard' principle was at work, for many landowners invested heavily in railway schemes.

Of course, at another level, there was a more straightforward reason for their opposition. If a line actually ran close to a park, the cuttings and embankments would be visually intrusive, and detract from the 'natural' appearance of the designed landscape. Whatever the precise mixture of reasons, hostility to the railways could take extreme forms, as in the famous case of the seventh Earl of Harborough, who directed cannons at the surveyors of the Midland Railway at work on the edge of his park.[33]

Most railway companies were sensitive to the views of the landed elite and preferred to leave landscape parks well alone. Sometimes, however – and especially in the more undulating areas of England – the dictates of topography made it inevitable that a line would pass close to, or even through, a park. In such cases, great pains could be taken to reduce its visual effects. The original line of the Wye valley railway in the Peak District would have taken it close to Haddon Hall. The Duke of Rutland refused to support the proposal, and the route was altered. Fourteen years elapsed while alternatives were explored. The eventual route, opened in 1863, passed to the north of Haddon park hidden in a tunnel.[34] The sixth Duke of Devonshire similarly insisted that the proposed line through Chatsworth Park should be entirely tunnelled.[35]

The influence of great landowners often had a major effect on the line of a railway in this way, leading to expensive and otherwise quite unnecessary works of engineering. Thus, for example, at Watford (Hertfordshire), the most direct route of the London-Birmingham line (constructed in the 1830s) would have been down the valley of the river Gade, but this would have meant it passing through the Earl of Essex's park at Cassiobury, and close to Lord Clarendon's at The Grove. It therefore left the valley just to the north of these places, passing some way to the east through cuttings and a mile-long tunnel, construction of which cost many lives.[36] The same principle can also be seen in the line from Cambridge to Bishop's Stortford. Leaving Cambridge, it closely follows the valley of the river Cam until the park at Audley End, home of Lord Braybrooke, is approached. It then veers westwards, passing through a series of cuttings and tunnels before returning to the valley, safely out of sight of house or park. Local historians will be aware of similar examples in their own areas.

The parkland landscape had to be protected from such encroachments of modernity. And yet its own style and appearance was changing with the times. The new plant introductions, which caused such intense excitement in the horticultural world from the end of the previous century had, to some, obvious advantages for park design. In 1849 R. Glendinning wrote an article on 'The Introduction of New Coniferous Trees into Park Scenery'.

They (*Pinus insignis*, *Lambertiana*, *ponderosa*, etc.) not unfrequently make a growth of three feet and upwards in a season . . . What in a park can give expressions of dignity and grandeur surpassing the *Abies Douglasii*. The rapidity of its growth is quite marvellous.

Glendinning was obviously a fanatic:

A moments reflection must surely point out how desirable in all places it would be to substitute these noble and gigantic pines for the worthless Beech, Birch, Sycamores &c. which predominate by the acre in hundreds of instances.[37]

Some owners, such as the Verneys of Compton Verney near Kineton (Warwickshire) or the Maharajah Duleep Singh at Elveden (Suffolk), caught Glendinning's enthusiasm. But, in spite of both 'picturesque' ideas, which greatly favoured the use of pines, and the popularity of exotics in garden areas, the new introductions were so patently alien to the English scenery that they were used in parkland only sparingly, and then usually to supplement rather than replace the existing deciduous species. Most parks by the end of the century, however, had their 'token' specimen exotics.

The Wellingtonia (*Sequoiadendron giganteum*), introduced in 1853, seems to have been a particularly popular choice although the initial lack of understanding of the plant caused some embarrassing

mistakes. In spite of Curtis's description of it in 1854 as 'a vegetable monster; a gigantic tree attaining a height of more than 300' . . .',[38] it was widely believed to need care and shelter. It was, therefore, often planted within the arms of shelter belts, in close proximity to houses, or in the corners of walled gardens. Even the Royal Horticultural Society was not exempt from this misapprehension and planted one in the corner of its new walled gardens at Kensington in 1861, where it quickly outstripped surrounding planting.[39] Today specimens can be easily identified, towering above all other parkland trees, much more intrusive in the landscape than their planters can ever have envisaged.

Landowners may have been reluctant to establish exotics in open parkland to any great extent, but they found a range of other

46 *Bicton (Devon): the Monkey Puzzle avenue, with the interplanting of 1977.*

uses for them. At Tresco, in the Isles of
Scilly, Augustus Smith planted an immense
windbreak of Monterey pines and
macrocarpas, extending over roughly 25ha
(60 acres), to shelter his gardens around the
Abbey in the 1830s.[40] The evergreen
introductions were a great improvement on
previous species used for shelter belts and, at
a time when privacy was uppermost in the
minds of many, were widely planted on the
perimeter of parkland.

The return to fashion of the avenue
provided designers with other situations in
which exotics could be displayed. The desire
to experiment with as many as possible
resulted in some unusual combinations.
Kew Gardens has a splendid example of a
mixed exotic avenue and at Madresfield
Court (Worcestershire), in the late 1860s,
intersecting avenues of golden yew, Atlantic
cedar and fir adorned the landscape.[41] The
most grandiose was, perhaps, that planted
by William Barron at Elvaston (Derbyshire)
in the 1830s:

. . . the first line of plants takes a wavy
direction . . . and is composed exclusively of
Irish Yews from 8 to 10 feet high. The first
straight line of plants to the rear of them consists
of *Araucaria imbricata*, alternated with *Picea nobilis*
and *Cryptomeria japonica*. The second row is
planted with Cedars of Lebanon and Deodars
alternately. The third line with *Pinus insignis*,
Douglas Firs, *Picea Webbiana*, *Abies Pinsapo* and
Hemlock Spruce.[42]

These were exceptions, however, and
single-species avenues were generally held
to be more pleasing. In 1842 Lady Rolle
planted the main approach at Bicton
(Devon) with *Araucaria araucana*. This still
exists and, although the trees are well past
their best, they were interplanted with
young specimens in 1977 to ensure the
avenue's future survival (Fig. 46). Monkey
Puzzle avenues were rare, but the fast
growth of the Wellingtonia ensured its wide
popularity for this kind of feature.

One of the most attractive aspects of the
ever-widening range of exotics was their
collectability and their potential for display.
Collections of exotic trees became a standard
feature of the country house landscape, even
on small estates although here they were
generally sited close to the house (Fig. 47).
At North Elmham (Norfolk), for example,
a low terrace in front of the hall, which
contained the formal bedding displays, was
extended to the west for nearly quarter of a
mile and planted with a range of exotic
shrubs and trees. On larger estates, where a
more extensive area around the house was
taken up with formal gardens, tree
collections were generally located further
away from the house, although they always
seem to have been regarded as an adjunct to
the pleasure-ground rather than as part of
the park.

Many of these were true arboreta and
pineta, in which the specimens were
organized according to their botanical
classification, or country of origin, each tree
standing separately and individually, and
often attractively labelled. Good surviving
examples are the collections at Nuneham
Courtenay (Oxfordshire) and Westonbirt
(Gloucestershire). The most magnificent,
perhaps, was that at Chatsworth, laid out by
Paxton in 1835. This extended over an area
of more than 15ha (37 acres) with the
specimens arranged in groups of 75 orders
comprising, in all, some 1670 species.
Paxton described all this in *The Gardener's
Magazine*:

It is laid out along both sides of a walk starting at
the front of the house, making a circuit of the
pleasure ground and finishing to the north-east
of the house near the old greenhouse and its
flower garden, a distance of about a mile in
length but with many bends due to the steep and
uneven ground.[43]

The success of all planting schemes
involving the extensive use of exotic
conifers was, however, dependent on local

47 *Thorpe Perrow (Yorkshire): the nineteenth-century pinetum adjoining the main garden terrace, incorporated into an extensive arboretum planted in the twentieth century and open to the public.*

climatic conditions. In the south–west the trees often flourished; on the drier eastern side of England, in areas prone to sharp late frosts, they tended to lose their foliage, bare out at the base, and quickly become thoroughly unsightly. They were soon removed, and replaced with more hardy alternatives.

Changes in the park did not just involve the more extensive use of exotic conifers. There was a proliferation in the number of walks leading out into the wider landscape from the pleasure-gardens, often threading through the perimeter belts of the park. There were various new features, sometimes designed to allow elements of the new taste for formality to be combined with the irregular, 'natural' appearance of the park. Thus, in particular, avenues were sometimes

planted, not with lines of individual trees spaced at regular intervals, but with small clumps spaced more irregularly down the line, in staggered rows. Looking down the feature, towards or away from the house, the appearance of an avenue was maintained. From the side, however, the clumps merged into the parkland scenery, and the feature became invisible (Figs 48 and 49).

Beyond the park the distinction between the native planting and the new wave of exotics could be used to advantage to display the extent of an estate; improved public mobility and access making this a matter of increasing importance. Alexander Forsyth was loud in his praise of Lord Vernon of Sudbury who planted 'thousands' of *Berberis aquifolium* as field hedges.[44] Apart from rhododendrons, whose tenacity to life is

48–9 *Clumped avenue at Heydon park (Norfolk). View A shows the vista maintained towards the house; View B the avenue viewed from the side. To compare the two views, note the positions of the dead tree stumps.*

notorious, the sort of plants Forsyth was talking about were relatively short-lived. The philosophy, however, is still evident at places such as Newby (Yorkshire), where purple beech adorn clumps of trees in what can only be described as decorated farmland.

There were, therefore, changes in the park and the wider landscape. But the greatest change of all was in the area immediately around the country house. As already noted, the garden returned with a vengeance. Yet, at the same time, landowners were reluctant to lose their cherished views of the park, which still retained its status as the quintessential symbol of gentility. This was one of the reasons why terraces, arranged

across the main facade of the house, remained popular throughout the century. For the smaller country house, the small terraced area with formal beds, or a single raised terrace, was often sufficient. But for the greatest landowners something rather grander was necessary and massive Italianate designs, richly embellished with architectural details, came once more into vogue.

At places such as Somerleyton (Suffolk), Holkham (Norfolk) or Trentham (Staffordshire), where the flatness of the land severely restricted the possibilities of this kind of design, vast open terraces with stone balustrading, urns and other decorations were created in front of the main facade of the house: smaller, subsidiary gardens led off from one side. Where the house stood on anything approaching a reasonable slope, however, the Italianate really came into its own, as at Shrublands (Suffolk), designed by Sir Charles Barry, with its monumental flights of stone.[45] Here, as elsewhere, the openness of the view was accentuated by the low growth of the bedding plants on the terrace itself. It is easy to appreciate the attraction of such designs to a generation brought up surrounded by landscape parks. Gardens further along the nearly mile-long terrace at Shrublands, and away from the direct view from the house windows, were more enclosed and sheltered, and contained a much greater variety of ornament and planting. An acceptable compromise of formal and informal, of open and enclosed, had been reached.

There were other ways in which the new popularity of the garden could be combined with the retention of views over open parkland. Occasionally, the ornamental gardens were simply located away from the house itself, separated by an area of open park. At Bicton (Devon), for example, a new house was completed for Lord Rolle in 1800,[46] considerably to the north of the building it replaced. The new house was

50 *Bicton (Devon): the palm house, erected c.1820 in the formal walled gardens to the south-east of the house.*

surrounded by parkland but the area of gardens designed for the earlier house was retained and, from as early as the 1820s, these were subjected to an extensive programme of addition and improvement (Fig. 50). The expense lavished upon them throughout the nineteenth century (the bill for garden labour alone was over £600 in 1880[47]) shows clearly that they were a valued feature in the design. Bicton became one of the most celebrated landscapes in Devon during the nineteenth century but the formal garden was separated from the house by over half a kilometre (third of a mile) of open parkland, and a lake. Their distance from the house must often have been

regretted by family and visitors alike.

It is almost impossible to describe a representative garden of this period. A kind of design anarchy prevailed. Theme gardens proliferated, following the example of Ashridge (Hertfordshire) where Repton laid out no less than fifteen.[48] Themes could be based on the geographical origin of plants, such as American or Chinese gardens, and suitably embellished with cultural accessories from whichever country was concerned. Or they could be produced the other way round, and plants of a (vaguely) suitable nationality selected to embellish a pagoda, or an Egyptian gateway. Alternatively the theme could be based on

51 *'Extraordinary effects in the borders': from a gardening magazine of 1885.*

associations, as in the Monks Garden at Ashridge, or might concentrate on particular genera of plants. Some plants were more widely used than others. Rosaries were almost universally popular throughout the period, at all social levels.

In gardens of great landowner and rural squire alike, garden buildings in all shapes and sizes could be found, from pagodas and rotundas to rustic summer-houses and gothic covered seats. Statuary and stonework were immensely popular, and rockwork grottoes and tunnels were considered particularly appropriate ornaments for fern and woodland gardens. There was considerable variation in the planting of new exotics. Some were simply confined to elaborate glasshouses but others were brought out 'for the season', and their pots sunk into the ground producing extraordinary effects in the borders (Fig. 51).

The transient nature of these, and of the new 'bedding plants', used in hundreds of unbelievably complicated patterns, meant that many features of the gardens changed year by year, and indeed throughout the year. Hardier exotic trees and shrubs were used singly on the lawns, to enliven borders and walks or to form exotic shrubberies. Topiary, mazes and a form of *parterre de broderie* returned to haunt the gardener, along with yew and box hedges in seemingly endless quantity. Shrubberies and woodland walks circuited practically everything, other than the house itself, and it would appear that the possibilities of garden design were only limited by the amount of paper available.

Many gardens of this period still survive in the landscape, although their layout has usually been considerably simplified in subsequent decades. In particular, while the 'hard landscaping' of paths and terraces often still exists in recognizable form, the flower-beds have usually been grassed over. Their layout is, however, often revealed during dry summers, in the form of parch-marks in the lawn in front of a country house. Such patterns are, like all parch-marks, most clearly seen from the air (Fig. 52). Vanished nineteenth-century flower beds are particularly visible in this way because, in many cases, they were created with remarkable thoroughness: at Audley End (Essex), for example, excavation has revealed that the beds of the cutwork parterre created in 1832 were excavated some 1.5m (5ft) into the subsoil.

52 *Houghton (Norfolk): traces of a late nineteenth-century parterre, revealed from the air as a pattern of parch-marks and shadows.*

6 'Beauty and utility'

The uses of parkland

Repton's ideal of combining 'beauty and utility' shaped the whole layout of late eighteenth- and nineteenth-century estate landscapes. Parks and gardens were there to be used, not just looked at, and the complex economic and recreational demands made upon them, rather than abstract ideas of art and fashion alone, moulded their appearance. One of the great advantages of the parkland landscape was that it allowed a diverse range of functions to be reconciled quite easily with aesthetic requirements, as can be seen with the use of parks for grazing. Parks had to be grazed, in order to maintain the smooth greensward; but at the same time, estate accounts make it clear that full economic advantage was taken of this. If the owner did not run sufficient stock in the park himself, then some or all of the grazing could be leased out, on a monthly, seasonal or annual basis. Sometimes, a number of local farmers contracted to run so many head of sheep and cattle within the park; sometimes, different areas within the park were leased out. The latter arrangement would obviously necessitate the maintenance of some internal boundaries within the park; indeed, any efficient exploitation of the grazing would have involved some measure of physical subdivision. Thus, although art historians might emphasize the uninterrupted sweeps of turf, in practice most parks were permanently divided up into sections, each separately named.

Ideally, internal divisions should have minimal impact on the landscape, and for this reason their boundaries were, to a large extent, defined by clumps and plantations.

---

53 *Examples of iron parkland fencing, from the catalogue produced by Boulton and Paul, Rose lane Works, Norwich, 1888.*

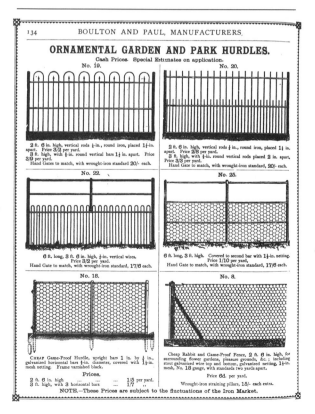

Indeed, the needs of grazing management could be a major influence on the layout of woodland areas, and it was probably for this reason that old perimeter belts were sometimes maintained as linear plantations within a newly-expanded park. But of course, fences did need to cross the open expanses of the park, and this could clash with the desire to have an open, uninterrupted swell of turf. Hedges would have been very visually disruptive, and would have made the park resemble the working agricultural land beyond the belt, something which was to be avoided at all costs. In the eighteenth and early nineteenth century, therefore, wooden hurdles or post-and-rail fencing were used, while later in the century, various kinds of iron fencing became available: firstly, iron tension fencing – 'invisible fencing', 'for gardens and pleasure grounds, where a light and airy appearance is more important than substantial workmanship';[1] and, from the 1880s, the kind of open park fencing still frequently seen in parks today, produced in vast quantities by firms like Messengers of Loughborough and Boulton and Paul of Norwich (Fig. 53). Originally valued because it tended to merge into the background, in time this kind of fencing came to be accepted simply because it was particularly associated with parks, and looked so different from the walls and hedges of the working countryside. By the end of the nineteenth century a range of ancillary ironwork features – gates, stiles etc. – were available, and can still often be found in parks.

Gates and stiles were necessary, because people did not merely look at the park out of the windows of the house. The landscape was there to be explored, by foot or on horseback. During the eighteenth century, paths for genteel promenading were usually restricted to the pleasure grounds in the immediate vicinity of the house. The park itself was for riding in, rather than walking

through. But towards the end of the century, paths were increasingly taken out into the parkland and woods, and there were often several 'delightful walks of communication . . . to increase the comfort of the place, while displaying its interesting features to advantage'.[2] In the summer of 1800 Thomas Staniforth and his wife visited their daughter and son-in-law at Restmorel Park in Cornwall. Thomas's diary noted his explorations of the grounds:

August 28 . . . in the afternoon I walked round the bath walk and returned by the lawn walk.

September 9 Walked with Mrs Hext . . . round by the Laurel Walk . . . after dinner I extended my walk over the church park to the reservoir.[3]

The circuit might take in the home farm, often constructed in a suitably ornamental fashion. A number of good examples can be seen at country houses which are open to the public, including John Soane's Park Farm, Wimpole (Cambridgeshire), and the elaborate Chinese Dairy built by Henry Holland at Woburn Abbey (Bedfordshire) in 1791 (Fig. 54). From the early nineteenth century, walks often extended out through the park belts, and although they were mostly abandoned long ago their traces can sometimes be found. They were frequently lined with box plants, which can survive for well over a century in woodland, although often in the form of great overgrown bushes, searching upwards for the light. Yew trees and thorn bushes also often mark the line of such paths, while iron gates and fences, buried in undergrowth, provide further clues.

Plantations had other functions in the complex landscape of the park: as areas for the production of wood and timber. Estate records provide a wealth of information about woodland management. They reveal that new plantations could be fiendishly difficult to establish. In particular, before the advent of wire netting in the 1830s, rabbits

54 *Woburn Abbey (Bedfordshire): the 'Chinese Dairy' designed by Henry Holland in 1791.*

were a terrible problem in many parts of the country. New plantations were sometimes protected by close-set chestnut paling, but often only with a turf bank, topped with gorse; payments to some elderly estate retainer for 'stopping the rabbit holes in the plantation banks' are often recorded in estate accounts. Such protection was often to no avail, as at Felbrigg (Norfolk), where in 1806 William Wyndham lamented 'The hares and rabbits destroyed the plantations on Harrisons Brake entirely, not withstanding the great cost of the fencing'.[4] Some of the plantations here had to be planted four times. In the absence of chemical controls weeds were another serious problem; potatoes were often sown before planting, in order to cleanse the ground.

Planting and after-care were, from the late eighteenth century at least, sometimes carried out by contract labour, with major nurseries like Fallas of Gateshead operating over a wide area. Such arrangements were not always satisfactory, as at Felbrigg, where in the 1820s William Wyndham grew increasingly dissatisfied with the service offered by Mackies of Norwich. 'It was well done, but cost too much money', he noted of a plantation in 1827. The following year he was less complimentary:

After the long trial and expense we have undergone, I never advise anyone to purchase trees of Mr Mackie.[5]

The plantations – which almost always included conifer 'nurses' for the hardwood trees – were planted very densely, often with more than one tree per square metre. This seems to have been done in order to suppress weed growth, and to allow for losses sustained from drought and the depredations of rabbits. But in addition it ensured a regular, if low, income from repeated thinnings of 'poles'. This was enough, according to some commentators, to pay the Poor Rate and the Tithes due from the ground in question, and to cover maintenance costs. The income derived from the sale of the larger timber taken from the later thinnings, and from the final clear felling, was thus pure profit.

Not all parkland woods were managed in this way. Some were coppiced, a traditional form of management by which deciduous trees were repeatedly cut down to a stump or stool every seven to ten years, in order to produce a regular crop of straight 'poles', suitable for minor building work, estate fencing, firewood and a host of other uses. Some areas of outgrown, long-abandoned coppice found within park belts represent blocks of ancient woodland, older than the park itself, incorporated within the designed landscape when it was first laid out. But others represent new areas of coppice established in the eighteenth and nineteenth centuries. These differed from the mixed underwood of traditional woods in that they are mostly composed of a single species, usually hazel or sweet chestnut.

Sale particulars from the late eighteenth century onwards graphically illustrate the way in which park woodland was both an aesthetic feature, and a commercial proposition. West Tofts in the Norfolk Breckland had a massive, near-continuous perimeter belt. A broad drive ran through the centre of this, which the catalogue described as a 'most agreeable drive or ride'. But, like all similar rides, it also had a practical function, providing access to the plantation for the extraction of wood and timber:

The Number of Trees which will remain . . .
after they are thinned so as to leave them at a proper Distance, to facilitate their Growth, will be about Six Hundred Thousand: which, in the Course of a few years, will at least be worth a Shilling a Tree, and consequently amount to Thirty Thousand pounds.[6]

This is an exaggeration, no doubt, like all estate agents' descriptions. Yet there can be no doubt that on marginal land, tree-planting on this scale offered a better financial return in the medium term than agricultural rents.

Commercial forestry was a more important feature of larger parks than of the smaller designed landscapes, where coppicing, thinning and felling would have been more visually intrusive. Even in the larger parks, however, there was always a potential conflict between aesthetics and economics. Rampant felling could entirely alter the appearance and structure of a design, but a family down on its luck might be forced to extract even the more visible and ornamental timber. Felling could be contemplated for other reasons. John Hobart, owner of Blickling (Norfolk), was ambassador in Moscow during the 1760s, and wrote a number of foul and bickering letters to his wife.

You say you go to take the air in the park not from inclination . . . but by order. This is a very puzzling and hurtful declaration indeed, to a man who is draining his pocket . . . to make his place agreeable and interesting to the eye. Write me such another word and I will turn every tree within a mile of Blickling into ready money.[7]

In general, however, aesthetics and the needs of forestry could be reconciled. The more commercial areas of woodland were located in the peripheral areas of the park, where clear felling and replanting could occur without ruining the view. The more visible trees, especially those in the open parkland, were usually only cut down if dangerous, diseased or dead, while the timber nearest the house was always considered exclusively in aesthetic terms. Here the most ornamental trees, and the more obscure exotics, were grown: trees that were both difficult to propagate and of minimal commercial value.

Timber management needed to be reconciled with aesthetics; both had to go hand in hand with the requirements of game. For parks in the eighteenth and nineteenth century never entirely lost their original function as killing grounds and larders. The principal quarry was now the pheasant, and its requirements had to be taken into account by designers and owners. Repton objected to narrow perimeter belts with a wide drive through the centre on the grounds that two narrow slips of plantation would not be 'such effectual harbours for game, as deeper masses; especially where the game is liable to be disturbed by a drive betwixt them'.[8] Writers like Alexander Forsyth, gardener to the Earl of Shrewsbury at Alton Towers, provided detailed advice on the shrubs and trees which should be planted in, and around, the park, to provide a suitable environment for game. In his treatise on 'Game Preserves and Fences' he prophesized that:

The crowning plant for game cover, the Rhododendron, which has hitherto been confined to small and expensive patches of the flower garden and shrubbery, now seems destined to skirt the moss and moorland for miles.[9]

A prophecy which has now come to be fully realized. Other plants he advocated 'not only to yield shelter and a hiding place for game but moreover supply food' included gorse, the more exotic *Pernettya mucronata*, *Mahonia spp.* and *Cotoneaster microphylla*. But rhododendron and snowberry (*Symphoricarpos rivularis*) are the most frequently encountered relics of game planting in parkland woods.

Combinations of hunting needs and aesthetics could occasionally take very complex forms. In 1788 the Duke of Newcastle set out a magnificent plantation on Apley Head, just outside Clumber Park.[10] A monument erected to the memory of his wife stood at the centre of 41ha (100 acres) of ornamental planting, laid out in the form of a goose foot in twelve divisions. The open vistas were separated by triangular plantations, each laid out in a number of blocks containing different species, with as many as twenty different sorts to each plantation. Curving shooting rides swept between groups of Balm of Gilead fir, horse chestnut, mountain ash and Weymouth pine, while borders of mixed shrubs provided cover and food for game.

Like parkland plantations, lakes had a variety of functions, besides being an essential element of the 'Brownian' park. They were used for sport and recreation, and many eighteenth- and nineteenth-century illustrations show people boating and fishing (Fig. 55). Boathouses – in various states of decay – can often be found beside lakes, although most surviving examples are of later nineteenth- or twentieth-century date. Lakes also supplied fish for the table, and sometimes water for the mansion. From the 1860s, many estates possessed a hydraulic ram, a form of pump which can use the power derived from a small fall in water to lift a fraction of the total flow to a greater height, a clever device invented by Montgolfier (of ballooning fame) in 1793. The ruined brick shells of these features can often be found near the dam retaining a parkland lake.

Ice houses were usually sited reasonably near the lake but discreetly hidden in (and shaded by) woodland or shrubbery. They were introduced into England in the late seventeenth century, and used to keep packed snow and ice, often collected from the lake in winter, for domestic use. They consisted of a deep cylindrical brick-lined pit, often internally domed, with an insulating mound of earth heaped over the

55 *Recreational use of parkland: boating on the lake at Heveningham Hall (Suffolk), from William Watt's* Seats of the Nobility and Gentry, *1779.*

top. Access was usually from the side, along a passage sealed with one or more doors, but there were many variations. Most ice houses are now ruined, and often dangerous to enter.

The landscape park thus had a complex range of functions, many of them essentially practical and economic. The pleasure-grounds in the immediate vicinity of the great house, in contrast, were purely aesthetic and recreational. There was another important difference between the two areas. Whereas the layout of the park tended to change slowly, that of the pleasure-grounds was much more frequently altered. While the ornamental trees here were usually retained with each change of fashion, the details of successive designs usually depended on flowering plants which had a comparatively short life, and which were frequently replaced with new layouts and varieties. As a result, the only surviving features of a Brownian or Reptonian pleasure-ground might be a scatter of yew trees, standing amidst much more recent planting. Even the layout of gravel paths within the pleasure-ground might change rapidly, although earlier arrangements can often be discerned in variations in the levels of the lawn, or are revealed by parch-marks visible in dry weather.

The kitchen garden

The kitchen garden, however, is different
again. This, like the park, combined 'beauty
and utility' in a subtle and complex way.
Many examples survive today, in various
states of decay. They are fascinating
complexes which have often been neglected
by garden historians.

Most kitchen gardens were walled on all
sides. Brick or stone was preferred but on
less affluent estates, well into the nineteenth
century, mud walling was occasionally
employed. Walls of all kinds were coped,
usually with tile or shaped brick, in order to
protect them from water penetration and
subsequent frost damage. Early kitchen
gardens formed part of the complex of
walled enclosures around a country house.
Often, as we have seen, they were not
clearly segregated, spatially or functionally,
from the other gardens. But on the largest
estates a growing separation is apparent
from the seventeenth century, if not before,
and more specialized areas of fruit and
vegetable production evolved. These were
often sited close to the stables, in order to
reduce the distance that manure had to be
barrowed.

In the early eighteenth century, a further
degree of segregation became normal on
large estates, as – with the development of
the 'late geometric garden' – walled gardens
of any kind fell out of favour, and designed
landscapes became larger and more open. At
places like Blenheim Palace and Wroxton
Abbey (Oxfordshire), kitchen gardens were
isolated some way from the house, on the
margins of the main garden areas (Fig. 56).
This tendency for isolation increased with
the development of the landscape park in the
second half of the century, although the
kitchen garden 'lost in the recesses of the
park' was never as ubiquitous as some books
suggest. Few visitors to country houses
would have been advised, as were those to
Chatsworth in the middle of the nineteenth
century, to take a carriage between the
house and the kitchen gardens.[11] Most
owners, particularly those of medium or
small estates, preferred to put convenience
first and kept the kitchen garden within easy
walking distance of the house, although it
was moved out of sight of the main facade
whenever possible, and was usually located
beside the stables and offices. Sometimes
this relative isolation was achieved, not
by moving the garden itself, but by
demolishing the other walled courts which
had hitherto connected it to the walls of the
house, as at Eaton (Cheshire).

Walled enclosures did not fit in with the
aesthetic of the open parkland, but this does
not mean that kitchen gardens were
considered unattractive. Indeed, the
importance of these areas for pleasure and
promenade is clear from numerous accounts
in diaries and letters. In the early 1800s
Charles MacIntosh, head gardener at
Claremont, saw the well-kept kitchen
garden as the rationale behind
'. . . conducting a stranger through the
labyrinth of pleasure-ground'.[12]
Descriptions of kitchen gardens from the
late eighteenth century onwards make it
clear that they often contained borders of
flowers, and while of course these do not
survive, many of the features which do
betray a subtle blend of use and ornament;
patterns of coloured bricks in walls,
ornamental wall coping, decorative path
edgings, and intricate cast-iron detailing on
glasshouses and gates. Even potting sheds
were sometimes given gothic window and
door details. Orangeries and summer-
houses can occasionally be found set into the

56 *Blenheim, Palace (Oxfordshire): an illustration
from Colen Campbell's illustration in* Vitruvius
Britannicus, *1725. The second area labelled 'B', to
the left, is the isolated kitchen garden.*

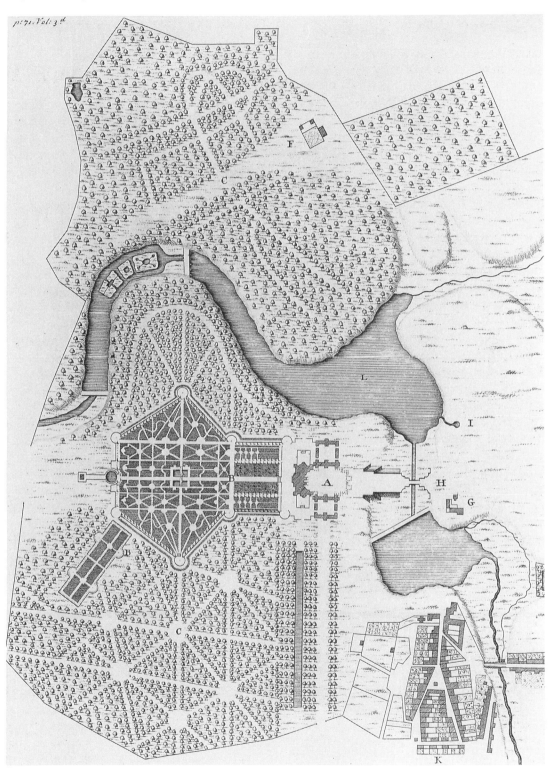

p:71.Vol:3.d

external walls. Fruit trees within the garden were trained in complex ways, partly for practical reasons, but also for aesthetic effect, and the dwarf box hedges defining the edges of paths were as much to give the garden a neat and formal appearance as to protect the plants in the adjacent beds.

The dominant aesthetic was one of efficient production. The kitchen garden provided an arena for the display of horticultural innovation, and for technological experiment. Thus, freed from the constraints imposed by the outline of adjoining enclosures, owners could experiment with the garden's shape, and a variety of plans developed. Gardens of square or rectangular form were always the most common, but there was often a slight distortion of this basic shape in order to provide longer south-facing walls (suitable for growing the less hardy and more prized varieties). Sometimes a more regular trapezoid form emerged, as at Raynham (Norfolk), Dawleigh (Devon) or Eaton (Cheshire). Curved walls or sections of walls helped to minimize dark, damp corners, and were fairly common features, and occasionally gardens were built with a semi-circular north wall, giving them a plan in the form of a half-circle. Whatever the precise shape adopted, a site which sloped gently to the south was always considered the best, since this ensured that the ground drained freely, and that the plants gained the maximum benefit from the sun.

The role of the kitchen garden as an arena for display, as a place to grow specialized and exotic produce, meant that the area it covered was only partially determined by the size of the household (including both family and servants) that it had to feed. MacIntosh in 1830 noted that some kitchen gardens exceeded 12 acres, but considered that 5 or 6 acres would 'if properly managed be found to afford sufficient vegetables for a family of the first class'.[13] Most members of the local gentry, however, had between one

and two acres of walled kitchen garden. Yet this often formed only part of the productive gardens on an estate.

At larger mansions, in particular, forcing grounds, frame yards, slips (areas surrounded by low walls, adjoining the garden proper) and orchards could usually be found in the vicinity of the kitchen garden, and there were – especially in the nineteenth century – extensive external ranges of sheds and stores.[14] These were usually built against the north side of the north wall, the darkest and most unproductive growing area. Here boiler houses, potting sheds, coke stores and tool houses can usually be found, in various states of dilapidation (Fig. 57). Brick-built sheds for storing fruit can also be discovered in such places, although often these were sited in more open, drier locations. In the late nineteenth century there was a vogue for building fruit stores of reed and thatch: known as 'Bunyard's fruit rooms', after the well-known Kent grower, George Bunyard (1841–1919). Few of these structures have survived, although occasional examples can still be seen, as at Chilton Foliat (Berkshire) or Aldenham House (now Haberdashers' Aske's School in Hertfordshire).

The gardeners were housed as close to the kitchen garden as possible, so that they could be on hand for tasks such as the stoking of the boilers, watering and opening of glasshouse lights; tasks which could not be confined to weekday working and daylight hours. The head- (and sometimes under-) gardeners were given separate houses, often built into the corners of the garden where they formed an important element in its design. The others might be housed in a dormitory or 'bothy', usually built against the outside of a wall. Examples of these low, cramped structures still sometimes survive.

The most important surviving feature of the eighteenth- or nineteenth-century kitchen garden are, of course, the walls

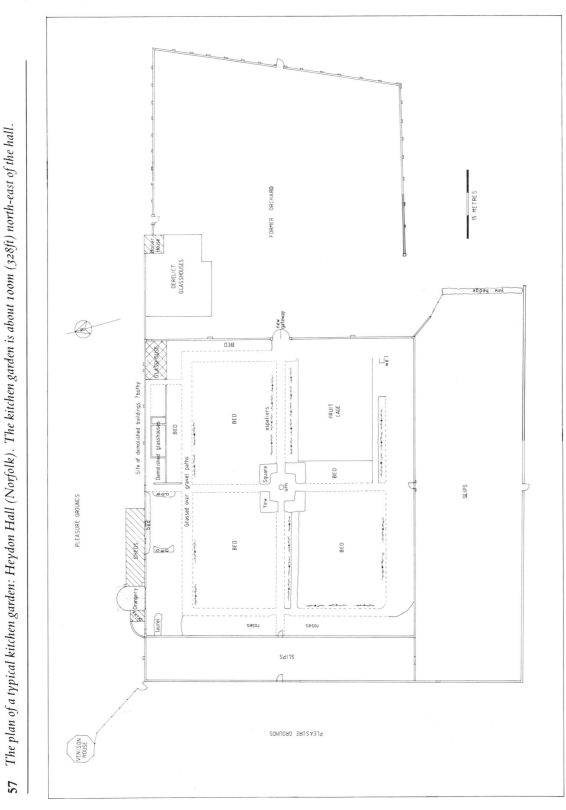

57 The plan of a typical kitchen garden: Heydon Hall (Norfolk). The kitchen garden is about 100m (328ft) north-east of the hall.

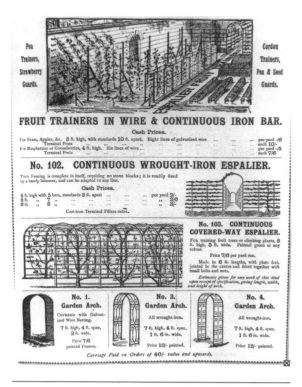

58 *Examples of espalier frames and arches, from the catalogue produced by Boulton and Paul, Rose lane Works, Norwich, 1888.*

themselves. Their main function was to provide protection for the plants growing within the garden: they were also used to support and ripen a wide range of fruit – apples, pears, peaches, nectarines, apricots etc. – in apparently endless variety. Both the external as well as the internal walls were used for this purpose, and occasionally short walls were extended outwards, at an oblique angle, from the exterior corners of the enclosure, in order to provide additional shelter for fruit. Piers and alcoves, on both the inside and outside of the wall, gave protection for fruit trees, as well as support and decoration for the walls themselves. Dwarf varieties of fruit trees were interspersed with full-height specimens, and both were trained into espaliers – regular

shapes. Their branches were tied in place with short lengths of cloth, nailed to the walls; the traces of this treatment are still evident in the numerous pock-marks in the garden walls. Espaliers were also trained on frames erected inside the garden, usually along the edge of the paths. Initially these were of wood, but in the nineteenth century, frameworks of metal rails and wires became available, together with arches and tunnels of open ironwork (Fig. 58).

Fruit could be made to ripen early by the use of 'Hot Walls'. These were hollow, with a series of internal ducts or flues. Hot air was circulated from a fireplace set into the base of the wall, or from a boiler on the outside. Temperature control was, however, rather difficult and care had to be taken to prevent damage to fruit and foliage from over-heating. The 'conservative wall' provided a rather more reliable method of ripening fruit. A permanent sloping glass roof was built out from the wall with huge, vertical glass slides, enabling whole sections to be opened, and moved on runners at top and bottom. A splendid nineteenth-century example can still be seen at Somerleyton (Suffolk) (Fig. 59). Simpler versions were made with cast-iron brackets fixed to the wall, which supported glass frames (Fig. 60). These were more versatile than true conservative walls, since the brackets could also be used to support shutters or netting which could protect the trees from strong sunlight or frost. An early version of such an apparatus is illustrated in Richard Bradley's *New Improvements of Planting and Gardening* of 1726.[15]

It was, however, in the design of glasshouses that technology made its greatest impact. These could be either freestanding or lean-to, and nineteenth-century examples often survive. Where they do not, it is often possible to determine their size, location and number from surviving traces. Thus, for example, the position of lean-to houses is often indicated by the

59 *The nineteenth-century 'conservative wall' on the south side of the kitchen garden, Somerleyton Hall (Suffolk).*

profile of the garden's external wall, for this was often raised in sections to accommodate their height. This rear wall was also often rendered internally, and/or white-washed, in order to reflect the light, and this coating is usually slow to decay. The rectangular openings which provided the ventilation for lean-to structures can also often be seen high up in the garden wall. As with sheds and stores, the location of glasshouses usually followed a regular, and logical, pattern. Most were built on the south side of the north wall, where they received maximum sunlight. Some, usually the more ornamental, can also be found against the

60 *Remains of framing on a kitchen garden wall. In the centre of the wall can be seen the raised section which backed a now-demolished glasshouse.*

south side of the south wall, outside the garden proper, where they often formed part of the pleasure ground.

Although framed glass lean-to structures for 'forcing' fruit had been known in England since the early eighteenth century, it was not until the end of the century that glasshouses became common. And it was not until the nineteenth century that improvements in technology and design brought the cheap mass-produced houses which were to be the mainstay of the kitchen garden for the next hundred years. Like the orangeries they superseded, early glasshouses were custom-built, expensive, and often served more than one purpose. In 1786 George Stewart was commissioned to design a glasshouse for Matthew Brickdale at Monckton in Somerset. The surviving plan shows the centre of the house with '. . . a pit for bark when it is used as a hott

house' and a '. . . floor while used as a greenhouse'. The accompanying letter from Stewart explains

. . . herewith I send a design for your intended plant or hott house. I have endeavoured to contrive it to answer both purposes, agreeable to your wish . . . to make a pinery the floor will be taken up to the ground, carry'd away 4' deep and a wall built up to form the pitt for bark.[16]

Until the repeal of the glass-tax in the 1840s, small panes were cheaper than large ones and were often used in glasshouses, slotted into closely-spaced glazing bars (Fig. 61). Small panes were, moreover, less likely to be pitted and uneven, and therefore less prone to frost-damage, than large ones.[17]

The repeal of the glass-tax and improvements in the technology of glass and cast-iron manufacture encouraged the mass-production of glasshouses, and by the

61   *Early nineteenth-century glasshouse at Hoveton Hall (Norfolk). The section on the right carries the original narrow glazing bars; that on the left, rebuilt at a later date, has larger panes and glazing bars further apart.*

second half of the nineteenth century there was a bewildering choice. Different kinds of glasshouse were manufactured for a wide range of fruit and vegetables: peaches, melons, cucumbers, grapes, mushrooms, the list was almost endless. Each type was purported to hold some specific advantage for the produce in question. Careful inspection of surviving remains can often indicate the kinds of fruit or vegetable they were designed to shelter. Vineries can be recognized by the fact that their brick bases are pierced by low arches, which allowed the vines to be planted outside the house, and thus spread their roots widely. The vines were trained up the inside of the steeply sloping roof and vineries were almost always of lean-to form, because of their height. Cucumber houses, in contrast, while similarly sloped to gain maximum height for the long fruit, tended to be narrower and much lower. Cucumbers were also grown in 'pits', that is, houses sunk below ground level, as were melons, while 'pines' (pineapples) were grown in the centre of a low glasshouse with a shallow-pitched roof, on a raised, level base surrounded by a walkway. By the end of the nineteenth century, glasshouses of all kinds were often artificially heated. Hot water was generated in boiler houses (usually located outside the garden, against the north wall), and pumped through the main houses in 10cm (4in) pipes.

In reality, few people could afford the full range of glass, and what was grown in a particular glasshouse did not always follow the manufacturer's intention: like the dish of mushrooms, submitted to the Norfolk and Norwich Horticultural society in 1829 by its president Evans-Lombe '. . . grown on the back shelf of the vinery'.[18] Nevertheless, by the end of the nineteenth century, even quite modest estates had extensive ranges of glass. At Didlington (Norfolk) there was, according to the Sale Catalogue of 1910, a 'peach house in two sections, range of

vineries, palm house, centre house, orchard and nectarine house, and two ranges of six pit lights'.

Most large kitchen gardens, from the end of the eighteenth century, had at least one ornamental glasshouse. This might form the centrepiece of a range within the garden, or it might be located on the south side of the south wall, adjoining the pleasure-grounds. Such structures had a variety of uses. The exotic species grown in them provided cut flowers for the mansion, and potted flowering plants for the formal gardens. But they also housed collections of orchids, cacti, ferns and other exotics. They were often richly decorated, with patterned floor-tiling and ornamental floor grids (although these were also used in the more expensive produce houses). Such features often survive inside the low brick walls which once formed the base of the glasshouse, long after the wood and glass superstructure has disappeared.

Considerable care was taken to create the appropriate environment for displaying particular collections. In ferneries, for example, the rear and/or side walls were often faced with pieces of (usually volcanic) rock, and the ferns were planted in the crevices. These rocks can still be found sticking to the kitchen garden wall long after the fernery once built against it has been demolished (the occasional hardy fern can sometimes be found still clinging tenaciously as further evidence). Ferns need a damp environment and a system of pipes was sometimes used to maintain a continuous trickle of water down the walls. This flowed into a channel of water beside the walkway and these channels also sometimes survive.

Internally, the kitchen garden was usually divided into sections or 'quarters' by a series of paths. In the early seventeenth century these could be of grass, but gravel increasingly grew in popularity, and in the nineteenth century cinder ashes or road chippings were also occasionally used. Paths were, and still often are, edged with trained fruit espaliers or low box hedges.

A good supply of water was essential and a 'pumpe, well or cisterne which might flow continually with water' was the 'necessariest ornament', as Gervase Markham noted in 1614.[19] In seventeenth-century gardens, the kitchen ground often lay beside a formal bason or canal, but even in this period a 'dipping pond', located (for a combination of practical and aesthetic reasons) at the junction of the cross walks in the centre of the garden, usually formed the principal water supply. In the course of the nineteenth century more complex systems of water supply were developed. Iron cisterns are frequent discoveries, sometimes within glasshouses, where they collected rainwater from the roof through an ingenious series of pipes. Iron pumps, too, can often be seen within glasshouses or, more often, standing in clumps of weeds, marking the spot where a glasshouse once stood. The garden hose

and modern sprinkler system have, of course, rendered all these labour-intensive methods redundant.

The importance of the kitchen garden both for produce and for promenade made its shelter critical (Fig. 62). The high surrounding walls created a warm and sheltered environment, but in certain circumstances could produce wind turbulence within the garden, and this could be especially damaging to glasshouses. The low walls of adjacent slips helped to reduce this problem, but shelter belts provided better protection. These were planted with care; the trees could not be too dense or too close to the wall, and the south side of the garden was often left open, or only lightly planted, so as not obscure the sun. Conifers were generally used, in order to give all-year-round protection, but these were usually interspersed with hardwoods and, in some cases, with fruit trees. Such belts often formed part of the pleasure-ground, and were planted with shrubs, threaded with walks and dotted with seats.

The kitchen garden by the end of the nineteenth century was one of the most labour-intensive gardens in history. Small wonder that it is usually the part of the country house landscape now in greatest decay, as one part-time gardener struggles with work previously carried out by five, six or more men. The domestic freezer has made forcing obsolete; ornamental houses contain only next year's geraniums and the sections or quarters are put down to tennis courts, fir plantations and chicken runs. Glasshouses are often ruinous, once-neat box hedges are now disconnected bushes scattered along the edges of paths, and the occasional outgrown fig or espaliered apple or pear tree are often the sole representatives of the once ubiquitous wall fruit.

62   *Pleasure and promenade in the early nineteenth-century kitchen garden.*

7 Public parks and gardens

To most people, the word 'park' conjures up an image, not of the landscaped grounds of a genteel country house, but of recreational space in the heart of a town or city. Public parks began to appear in the nineteenth century, but public gardens in one form or another existed in England from at least the seventeenth century. These, not surprisingly, seem to have resembled contemporary private gardens. Indeed some, like those at Marylebone, developed from gardens which had originally surrounded private residences. This particular example was described by a visitor in 1650 as having gravel walks, both straight and circular, 'double set with quick set hedges, full grown and indented [castellated?] like town walls', and was surrounded by brick walls against which fruit trees were grown.[1] Cuper's garden at Lambeth was laid out on virgin meadow ground, and by 1691 boasted walks and arbours ornamented with statuary.[2] Visitors came to such places to walk, play bowls and generally enjoy the open air and peace away from the noise, smells and tumult of the city. Gardens like these seem to have drawn their clientele from all social classes. There were usually no admission charges, the owner deriving a profit from refreshments or other items sold on the premises.

In the seventeenth century commercial pleasure gardens were largely restricted to London. In the following century, however, as the 'consumer revolution' gathered pace,

they began to appear elsewhere. Important spa towns like Bath had elaborate layouts with fountains, canals and cascades which vied with those in London (Fig. 63), but more diminutive gardens could be found in

63 *Bagnigge Wells in London, in the early eighteenth century.*

most major urban centres. Music and dancing became standard attractions in even the smallest establishments, and a wide variety of pastimes and sports was usually on offer. In 1718 the Adam and Eve gardens at Tottenham had grounds for skittles and Dutch pins, a small menagerie and ponds with water birds and goldfish.[3] Illuminations were advertised at Marylebone from as early as 1718,[1] initiating the almost universal use of gardens in the evening as well as during the day. By the 1730s water sports were widely catered for with angling, swimming and ice-skating on offer at many establishments.[4] Fireworks became *de rigeur* from the 1740s, and mechanical devices, waterworks and grottoes grew in popularity, and concerts were regular features. The public garden was, by 1750, a very different place to the quiet refuge of a century before. It had more people, more activity and more noise.

This was not the only way in which such gardens had changed. The earlier mix of classes seems, to some extent, to have been replaced by a greater degree of social segregation. Many of the larger gardens began to charge for admission, and this was probably intended to maintain social exclusivity as much as to generate extra income. Islington Spa in 1733 enjoyed royal patronage but also socially mixed company; by 1750 the charge for admission was 1s 6d and the clientele select.[5] Marylebone charged 1s for admission from 1737, and by 1753 could boast 'the largest and politest assembly', although by 1760 here, as elsewhere, 'genteel persons could walk gratis'.[1] Many other gardens, however, catered for a less exalted clientele, and were sporadically a target for public order legislation. An Act of 1752, imposed on the area within 20 miles of London, required that all places where music and dancing were offered should be licensed. Magistrates could refuse to license those deemed to be a public nuisance. As might be expected, the

law was rarely enforced in the haunts of the rich. Indeed, one of the stated intentions of the Act was to 'correct, as far as possible, the habits of idleness of the lower orders'.[6]

Increasing social segregation went hand in hand with a further proliferation in the number of pleasure gardens which could now be found in most towns and cities.[7] Whatever the nature of their clientele, their layout continued to be highly geometric, apparently little affected by the trend towards naturalism and irregularity which was sweeping the grounds of the country house. In 1774, the gardens at White Conduit House in London had 'prettily disposed walks with a pond in the centre and an avenue of trees with genteel boxes set into hedges';[8] Cromwell's Gardens, opened in 1776 and the haunt of 'fashionable gentlemen', had neatly-kept grounds containing arbours and 'curiously cut trees' surrounding an elevated lawn;[9] while the Temple of Flora, visited by 'persons of good position' when opened in 1788, advertised cascades, fountains, waterworks and statuary among its many attractions.[10]

It may seem surprising that the affluent classes continued to relish such geometric delights long after they had been banished from the immediate vicinity of country houses. But relish them they did. Partly, of course, the retention of such features was related to the way in which these areas were used. An essentially geometric structure was eminently suitable for the diverse range of activities which these gardens had to accommodate. Thus hedged enclosures provided spaces and compartments for a range of games or performances, while gravel paths provided an arena for promenading and display. But in addition, the retention of geometry may have been related to the space available. Most commercial pleasure grounds covered an area of between 1 and 5 acres and even Vauxhall's 12 acres (one of the favourite haunts of the Prince of Wales[11]) were hardly

64 *Vauxhall Gardens, London, c.1750.*

sufficient for the sweeping grandeur of the landscape park (Fig. 64).

Some much larger areas for public recreation did, however, exist by this time, at least in the metropolis. Some of the royal parks in London had been open to the public from at least the time of Charles I.[12] Here, too, there is evidence for social segregation. Belsize Park was opened to the 'public' in 1720, but descriptions make it clear that it was mainly used by the gentry and nobility, for deer hunting, racing and gambling.[13] In 1727, a visitor waxed lyrical about the kinds of people visiting St James Park:

What can be more glorious than to view the body of the nobility of our three kingdoms in so short a compass, especially when freed from mixed crowds of savoy fops and city gentry?[14]

Some level of social exclusivity was maintained in most royal parks around London throughout the eighteenth century: in 1780 'quality' were admitted freely to Hyde Park but the poor and shabby were excluded.[15] But the increasing importance of the urban middle classes constituted a different kind of problem. William Boulton, writing in the early nineteenth century, recalled how the elite forsook the delights of St James Park:

About 1786 fashion left its shades and avenues to the middle classes, the city ladies and the country cousins and moved off unaccountably to Green Park.[16]

The driving wedge of the middle classes, combined with the increasingly crowded and violent nature of London, ensured that from the end of the century, the very rich progressively forsook its public promenades and pleasure grounds, and increasingly created a social life which was largely based on reciprocal visits to country estates.

The early nineteenth century – the middle-class park

Commercial interests were not slow to exploit the increasing affluence, and size, of the urban middle classes. It was they, rather than society as a whole, for whom 'public' parks, botanic gardens and cemetery gardens were created in the first half of the nineteenth century. There was, initially at least, no intention that these should be available to everyone. Public parks were for a particular section of the 'public'; their fences, gates and lodges betrayed their segregational aims in the same way as those of the private landscape park. Indeed, the earliest urban parks were primarily intended as adjuncts to middle-class housing schemes. Prosperous industrialists, financiers, and civil servants who had to live for much or all of their time in cities wanted good-quality housing in pleasant and exclusive surroundings. Such people were not in a position to afford a private parkland landscape; but they were anxious to have a share in one.

In 1811 Marylebone Park, soon to become Regent's Park, was Crown property but leased to the Duke of Portland. The lease was due for reversion in that year and the Prince Regent, like many other owners of free space in cities, wanted to develop the area for building. A development plan for the park had already been prepared by John White in 1809 (Fig. 65).[17] White carefully avoided building over the whole area of the park. A central core of landscaped parkland was to be maintained, and surrounded by a ring of substantial houses, some detached and some semi-detached. These faced on to

a carriage-drive, which ran all around the park's perimeter. All the houses had a view on to the park, and free access to it. In the event, this plan was abandoned in favour of one drawn up by the architect John Nash in 1811.[18] Subjectively, this seems a more pleasing design, but its acceptance in preference to White's proposals was probably due to economic rather than aesthetic considerations. It proposed the erection of terraced residences, rather than detached and semi-detached houses, around the periphery of the park, thus increasing the density of dwellings on offer. In addition, a scatter of exclusive detached residences was to be built within the park, each set in 8ha (20 acres) of private grounds. The reduction in the overall area of the parkland involved in this second design was, to some extent, compensated for by the provision of a much more varied landscape, with a lake, canal and skilfully arranged trees.

The Times of 1829 bemoaned the fact that the result of Nash's plan was 'no longer a

65 *Plan of Marylebone Park, London, by John White.*

park but an irregular polygon of buildings with grass and water in the midst of it'.[19] Regent's Park was, in effect, an up-market housing estate, and although officially open to the public, part was still kept as a subscription garden.[20] Even the 'public' area seems to have been a fairly exclusive space: in 1823 Peter Joseph Lenne could write that it was necessary to be a man of fortune, and to take exercise in a carriage or on horseback, in order to enjoy Regents Park[21] and Nesfield's illustration of the park, made in 1863, shows only multitudes of the fashionably-dressed.[22]

The basic structure of Nash's design, as accepted by the Prince and his advisers, largely survives today, although much was added later in the nineteenth century: flower beds, recreation areas, and botanical and zoological gardens, all illustrating the changing demands made on urban parks in subsequent decades.

Developments like Regent's Park were not confined to the metropolis. In 1843 Royal Assent was given to the Third Improvement Act which empowered the purchase of 226 acres of land in Birkenhead for development, 125 acres of which were to be dedicated for public recreation in perpetuity.[23] The design for this new park was by Joseph Paxton, and it included all the features fashionable in contemporary private parks and gardens, suitably adapted to the unpropitious, low-lying nature of the site, and to the needs of public recreation: lakes with naturalistic curves, partially fringed, but not too heavily, with trees; careful planting to provide a constant element of surprise to the promenader, and to disguise the true extent of the design. But where the private park would have had a perimeter belt of trees, Birkenhead had a belt of upper-middle-class housing. It was the sale of these 'handsome and well-built villas' which provided the money necessary for the purchase and construction of the park; the park, conversely, added to the value of the

66 *'The language of exclusion'. The main gateway, Birkenhead Park.*

houses that overlooked it, for it was emphasized that the fashionable villas commanded 'as fine a view as though each were set in its own park'.[24] They were certainly positioned in such a way that they effectively blocked any other views into Paxton's elegant landscape.

Birkenhead still provides a fine example of Paxton's ability as a designer. The park survives in a reasonable condition, although some of Paxton's original buildings are now in a rather poor state of repair. The ornamental rockwork which was positioned at many of the main path intersections – made from material excavated from the lake – remains a notable feature.

The often-repeated claim that Birkenhead was the first park bought by the people, for the people, needs to be treated with a measure of scepticism. Its main function was to serve the aims of developers and the ambitions of the affluent middle classes. Its use as a public open space was secondary. The same was largely true of the other urban parks developed in the early and middle decades of the century, such as Pennethorne's Victoria Park (London), of 1841, or Paxton's Princes Park (Liverpool), of 1843. All mirrored Regent's and Birkenhead Parks in their broad framework: 'naturalistic' parkland, cordon of respectable houses, carriage-drive, lodge and gates. It was the language of exclusion; a language the poor understood only too well (Fig. 66).

Public parks in the late nineteenth century: control and philanthropy

The interests of the middle classes in more exclusive grounds left the older-style commercial pleasure-gardens free for less select company: increasingly, they were the resort of the lower middle classes and the urban workers. In 1810, Bagnigge Wells in London was said to have become exclusively the resort of the lower classes; White Conduit House had 'odd company' in 1826, when magistrates attempted to close it.[25] They failed to do this – it was still offering varied entertainments in the 1840s – and many similar establishments continued to provide, into the 1850s and beyond, much the same range of diversions as had been on offer a century before. Page's Greyhound Gardens in Norwich was typical. It had terrace walks, arcades and grottoes, three resident bands, rope dancing and fireworks to delight early nineteenth-century visitors.[26] The first canary show in the country was held there in 1846.[27] In 1858 Highbury Barn in London boasted bowers, alcoves, and an avenue of trees with statue lights, musical entertainments and a dancing platform. Noise and bad behaviour brought sustained opposition from local residents, but it remained open until 1871.[28] Private and official opposition were common, and part of a general attempt to regulate working-class activities by controlling the spaces in which they took place.

Not all such spaces were commercial pleasure-grounds, however. Unenclosed commons and heaths on the margins of the larger towns and cities were places of informal recreation, used for prize fights, gambling and protest meetings. The enclosure of such areas in the early nineteenth century was often motivated as much by considerations of public order as by any economic benefits to be gained by the owners, who were often the governing corporations of the towns in question. Significantly, there were sometimes attempts to turn them into more controllable public open spaces. The corporation of Preston enclosed an area of open land to create Moor Park in 1834: but, although lodges were built and the perimeter bordered by roads, the area within remained unplanted for nearly thirty years.[29] Attempts to change the character of open spaces in this way could, on occasions, meet with fierce local opposition.[30] Mousehold Heath lay outside the city walls of Norwich and, together with the adjacent hamlet, was held by the more 'respectable' elements of local society to be lawless and violent. In addition to enjoying prize fights and other entertainments, the local community were illegally exploiting the mineral rights on a substantial scale. Frustrated in their attempts to curtail such activities, in 1864 the Dean and Chapter of Norwich cathedral – owners of the land – offered the heath to the Sheriff of Norwich on the condition that it was turned into a 'People's Park'. Substantial levels of opposition ensued: the plan failed, and it was not until 1884 that a body of 12 conservators was established, and provisions for improvements made, which included tree planting, the erection of lodges and the provision of regular policing. Even this plan was, in the event, only partially carried out.[31]

Difficulties and delays like these were common in the provision of ordered public parks. Thus, for example, H.P. Hornor suggested as early as 1849 to the Liverpool Improvement Committee that 'a belt of garden or parkland bounding the present extent of the town' should be established. But it was not until the 1870s that such parks came to be established on the city's periphery.[32] For although there was pressure from social reformers to provide public open spaces for the urban poor, middle-class residents were often less enthusiastic. In 1847 Manchester Corporation proudly unveiled three new parks: Peel, Queen's, and Philips. All were fairly small, covering around 12ha (30 acres); and all, like Birkenhead, were principally intended as the centrepieces for middle-class housing developments. But in this case, the corporation took the unusual step of providing areas within them for public games and sports, a measure which caused much local opposition. This was in spite of the fact that the areas allotted for such recreational use were carefully sited in discreet recesses, or enclosed by hedges, so that they would not intrude on the enjoyment of more sedate citizens. There were complaints about 'men shouting', and the 'unrestrained merriment of the factory girls'.[33] The sports ground was removed from Philips Park only two years after it had been opened.

There was insufficient middle-class support for such developments to be politically feasible on a large scale in the middle decades of the century, and most of the truly public open spaces established in this period owed their creation to the initiatives of prominent local philanthropists. The arboretum created by Joseph Strutt in Derby, and opened in 1840, is one of the earliest examples. The design was by J.C. Loudon; it was he who persuaded Strutt that a pleasure ground consisting simply of grass and trees would become insipid after a few visits, and would be of little educational value to the urban masses. He suggested instead an arboretum, embellished with serpentine walks, avenues, arbours, seats, statues and flower vases. Not all the area, however, was devoted to botanical education. Strutt insisted that two open spaces should be provided where bands could play, dancing take place and on which marquees could be pitched. But access was not entirely

unrestricted. The local working classes were to be admitted free on Sundays and one other day of the week; everyone else had to pay an admission fee.[34] The arboretum was a pleasant place – and indeed still is, although now with few of the original trees, and with its planting banks bare of shrubs. The gratitude expressed by the printers and bookbinders of Derby, on the commemorative inscription they presented to their benefactor, was no doubt genuine: they thanked him for 'opening these beautiful grounds on the day of rest from laborious employment to facilitate the . . . enjoyment of the working classes'.[35]

The inhabitants of many cities today have good reason to be grateful to philanthropists like Strutt. But their motives were seldom entirely altruistic. In 1857 Francis Crossley, prosperous carpet manufacturer, endowed Halifax with its 'People's Park'. This was fairly small, but was complete with bandstand, terracing and a fountain, and by 1859 public baths had been provided in the south-west corner. Crossley's father had worked his way up the social ladder from weaver to factory owner: his sons, by astute business dealings, had made Crossley Carpets a household word. For Francis Crossley and his brothers, endowment of Halifax with a range of facilities was a social duty; it also resulted in social advancement.

The ceremony which accompanied the opening of the park was lavish, featuring bands, a procession of local Temperance and Friendly Societies, and 3000 Crossley workers, each carrying a banner made of Crossley carpeting: an advertising opportunity, clearly, which was not to be missed.[36]

Belle Vue, the house Crossley built for himself in Halifax, overlooked the park and, before the planting matured, visually dominated it (Fig. 67); the parallel with the country house and its landscape is unavoidable. There was a statue of Crossley in the park, and suitable texts extolling his

67 *The People's Park, Halifax: from* The Illustrated London News, *22 August, 1857. The house in the top right corner is 'Belle Vue', the residence of Frank Crossley.*

generosity. But the path of upward mobility led away from Halifax; led, by 1862, to a baronetcy, and to the purchase of the Somerleyton estate, over 3000 acres in the Suffolk countryside, complete with newly-extended hall, and elaborate gardens designed by William Andrews Nesfield (see p. 38). Crossley was by then a millionaire; his son was educated at Eton.[37]

In the second half of the century, urban corporations began to take over from individual philanthropists as the main providers of public open spaces. This was one aspect of a more general increase in the involvement of local government in the provision of amenities, ranging from street-lighting to sewage disposal. National

government facilitated the provision of public open spaces with the passing of the Recreation Ground Act of 1859.[38] The motives of local and national government were mixed. At one level, there was genuine social concern, the desire to give the urban worker the opportunity for healthy recreation in pleasant surroundings. There was also a measure of civic pride, as neighbouring towns and their prominent families attempted to outdo the facilities provided by their neighbours. And there was the ideal of improvement: the desire to mould the urban worker into a well-ordered, healthy, respectable, if subordinate, citizen. But the proliferation of public parks was not universally welcomed,

68 *Spring Gardens, Buxton, from a railway guide to the Peak District, c.1902. The park was designed by Edward Milner.*

and opposition to their creation on the part of middle-class residents continued into the second half of the century. In 1872 the mayor of Leeds, John Barren, met with considerable local opposition when he attempted to establish a public park at Roundhay. His struggle was celebrated in the poem 'The Battle of Roundhay Park'. The 35 laboured verses include the following:

> The Council and the People
> United did agree
> That Roundhay Park just three miles off
> The People's Park should be
>
> But there uprose a mighty crowd
> As wealthy as they're proud
> Said they, 'This park's too beautiful
> For Leeds' vulgar crowd.

Says Tommy Greenwood, who was once
A working man you know
'What right have working men of Leeds
Into a park to go?

We men of wealth have got our grounds
In which we walk about
But shall we pay for such-like toys
For any dirty rout?[39]

Barren was successful, and everywhere the tide was turning.

The design of this multitude of new urban parks mirrored, to some extent, developments in contemporary country house landscapes; hardly surprising, perhaps, given that many designers, most notably Paxton and Kemp, worked on both. But the aesthetic of the pleasure ground was more dominant in these new urban landscapes than that of the landscape park.

Serpentine paths threaded between a variety of exotics, and elaborate bedding schemes were a prominent feature. The flood of new varieties of plants and the improvement in iron and glass technology in the second half of the nineteenth century led to infinite variations in internal design and buildings. Parks became more and more elaborate as borough vied with neighbouring borough to produce a fitting expression of its prosperity (Fig. 68).

In some ways, the intricate bedding displays, floral clocks, magnificent winter gardens and pavilions, were reminiscent of the extravagant eccentricities of the old commercial pleasure-grounds. They certainly struck a chord with the urban workers, who flocked to these new landscapes on Sundays and holidays. The commercial pleasure-grounds went into terminal decline from the 1860s, and the public parks took their place in the provision of sport and entertainment.

Examples of nineteenth-century parks abound in English towns and cities, although they have often been much altered by later developments. Good examples include Stanley Park, Liverpool, designed by Edward Kemp and laid out in the 1860s; Spring Gardens and the Serpentine Walks at Buxton; and there are many London examples, including the grounds laid out by Paxton around the Crystal Palace at Sydenham. Victorian ironwork, as well as much original planting, survives in many smaller urban parks: bandstands in particular are common features.

Parks continued to be added to the urban landscape in the twentieth century, and the inter-war years, in particular, often saw new parks formed as 'job-creation' schemes for the unemployed. Up until the Second World War municipal parks were considered a suitable venue for Sunday School outings and 'treats'; a place where the urban workers could 'don their best Sunday Clothes and disport themselves in a becoming manner'.[40]

They continue to develop, although since the war the emphasis has been more and more on sports and games, rather than on plants, trees and elaborate gardens; a trend which is accelerating with the increased squeeze on Local Authority budgets.

Cemetery gardens

The overcrowded and insanitary condition of urban churchyards had caused concern in England since the seventeenth century, and as early as 1711 the establishment of cemeteries on the outskirts of London had been proposed by Christopher Wren.[41] The problem was, however, exacerbated by the phenomenal increase in the size of many towns and cities in the eighteenth century. By the beginning of the nineteenth, the condition of urban graveyards was notorious, with – in some cases – bodies being exhumed to make way for more interments even before they had fully decomposed.[42] The only solution was the establishment of large, new cemeteries, but – as with the provision of public parks – systems of urban government, and of financing local administration, rendered any corporate solutions impossible before the middle decades of the nineteenth century.

Up until 1852, therefore, when Burial Boards were established, new cemeteries were entirely financed by private companies. The success of their ventures depended, above all, on attracting the most prestigious and wealthy customers, who would advertise their presence by the erection of flamboyant monuments on the most prominent, and therefore most expensive, sites, adorning the cemeteries and attracting further custom.

It ought to be a general rule to place handsome monuments at particular points of view . . . points seen from the entrances and from the chapels etc.[43]

Smaller, mass-produced monuments erected by those with less wealth occupied less expensive, and therefore less prominent plots. Those with no monuments, pauper graves paid for by the parish, were given the most marginal positions of all, often in separate enclosures outside the main area of ornamental grounds.

For these were indeed ornamental, aesthetic landscapes – true 'garden cemeteries'. The inspiration for this new form of designed landscape is said to have been the great cemetery established at Père Lachaise, outside Paris, in 1807, but although this was no doubt influential the idea of the garden cemetery had more complex roots.[44] A desire to commemorate the dead in a pleasant and evocative setting was evident among the wealthy from at least the early eighteenth century and it was a desire sanctioned by classical precedent. Alongside the statues and busts of classical poets and Roman emperors, monuments to the more recently dead sporadically made their appearance in parks and pleasure-grounds. Jonathen Tyers, proprietor of London's famous Vauxhall pleasure-garden from 1728, bought Denbies, near Dorking (Surrey), in 1734. He laid out the garden in fashionable style, with 'Alleys cut through woods and prospects', but the mood was sombre and the ornaments dedicated to truth, time and death. Some time in the 1740s he commissioned the sculptor Roubiliac to build a monument to his friend, Lord Petre. It was a vast, elaborate structure of stucco, a pyramid surmounted by an angel blowing the last trump.[45]

69 *Blickling Park (Norfolk): the mausoleum designed by Joseph Bonomi, 1793. The last resting place of John Hobart, second Earl of Buckinghamshire.*

This was one of several private monuments and mausolea erected by the rich within their private grounds. These included the great rotunda designed by Nicholas Hawksmoor for Lord Carlisle at Castle Howard; Wyatt's mausoleum at Cobham Park (Kent), erected in 1783; and that created by Joseph Bonomi for the second Earl of Buckingham at Blickling (Norfolk) (Fig. 69). Parks provided other opportunities for exclusive burial, in the form of the parish churches left isolated by the removal or destruction of their attendant villages. These became, in effect, part of the estate landscape. Indeed, the church was sometimes rebuilt or altered so that it resembled a garden building more than the spiritual centre of the community; most notably, perhaps, at Nuneham Courtenay, where the Earl of Harcourt replaced the original medieval structure with a domed classical edifice. Burial in such a feature, full of family monuments and isolated within a park, must have resembled interment in a private mausoleum. The park had provided exclusivity during life and, for some, it continued to do so even in death.

Not all monuments and mausolea, however were enshrined in the privacy of the landscape park; indeed usually the reverse. The memorial erected by the Duke of Newcastle to his wife, in the 1780s, was situated high on Apley Head, on the edge of Clumber Park;[46] Sir Francis Dashwood's mausoleum at West Wycombe (1764/5) was outside the park; and the Castle Howard mausoleum can be viewed for miles in several directions. The object of such memorials was that they should be visible and that 'the great' should continue to be revered even after their death. Families strove to place memorials in the highest and most dominant positions, and to draw public attention to them. At West Wycombe the line of a public road was altered specifically to focus on Dashwood's mausoleum; it is impressive even today.

Thus, in a number of ways, the eighteenth century forged powerful links between elite status and burial in a landscape or garden setting. These connections may have been as important as any foreign influences or examples in the development of the idea of the cemetery garden in the following century. Indeed, the styles that emerged for the new burial grounds closely mirrored those in private pleasure-ground design, drawing on a mixture of the landscape style and the ideas of the 'Picturesque' as developed by designers like Loudon. St James' cemetery in Liverpool, opened in 1829, is a superb example of the influence of the picturesque.[47] It occupied the area of a former quarry, the old working faces of which were cut to form catacombs and dramatic processional ramps for the funeral carriages. A temple-like structure, high above the quarry floor, served as a mortuary chapel and paths wound through densely-planted trees. The cemetery at Kensal Green, opened in 1833, by contrast, was more akin to a landscape park, with classical lodges and temples, serpentine drives and clump planting. It was so successful that two of George II's children, the Duke of Sussex and Princess Sophia, chose to be buried there in preference to the more traditional Windsor.[48]

The Builder magazine of 1862 described the Coventry cemetery, designed by Paxton and opened in 1847, in telling terms:

We approach an octagonal stone prospect tower on which a small notice board is fixed. This informs us it is the entrance of the cemetery. But for this notification we might have fallen into error, the place having much more the air of a gentleman's park than a city for the dead.[49]

The resemblance was not, of course, coincidental, nor was the remark intended as a criticism.

Those who advocated other forms of design for cemeteries had an uphill struggle. Some rather more formal and geometric layouts were created in the early nineteenth century, but these were usually small. The one really large example, at Brompton, was – perhaps significantly – poorly subscribed and, ultimately a financial disaster.[50] J.C. Loudon, who wrote extensively on the subject in the first half of the century, expressed his frustration over the popularity of cemeteries which aped the landscape of the country house so slavishly: 'That they are much frequented and admired by the public is no proof that they are in appropriate taste'.[51] He was adamant about what was, and what was not, acceptable:

Every mode of introducing trees and shrubs which is identical with that practised in planting parks and pleasure grounds is to be avoided, as tending to confound the character and expression of scenes which are, or ought to be essentially distinct.[52]

Loudon developed a specific 'cemetery style' as a foil to what he termed 'Picturesque, English Landscape, or Pleasure Ground Styles'.[53] This involved the planting of a wide but nevertheless carefully selected range of species (the list in his book ran to 20 pages).[54] These included numerous deciduous trees and flowering shrubs, such as Mock Orange, *Cydonia japonica*, *Chimonanthus fragrans*, and *Daphne mezereum*, as well as herbaceous flowers and bulbs. But Loudon mainly advocated evergreens, partly for reasons of maintenance (few leaves to be raked up in winter), but mainly for reasons of symbolism. His preferences were, on the whole, shared by most planters and designers, although many added the weeping willow to this list, a tree to which Loudon had a strong aversion. Loudon's taste in cemetery planting certainly fitted in well with the wave of new exotic evergreens flooding into the country in the first half of the nineteenth century. 'Why not have the deodar [introduced in 1831] in all our cemeteries and burial grounds?', asked

Robert Errington in 1850, 'Surely its weeping character carries a funereal cast . . .'[55] (Fig. 70). Rural churchyards also benefitted from this enthusiasm for evergreen planting. Yews had been planted within them since the Middle Ages, but enthusiastic encumbents now added Irish yew, juniper, cypress and cedar, usually along the main paths, or on the perimeter, where space was more freely available.

Loudon gave careful consideration to other aspects of planting which might make the cemetery a distinct form of landscape.

We would never plant flowers or flowering shrubs in the margins of masses or belts, or in beds or patches that might be mistaken for those of a lawn or flower garden; but to give them a distinctive character we would plant them in beds in the shape of graves or coffins.[56]

70 *The Rosary Cemetery, Norwich: any tree which carried a 'weeping caste' could be included in the repertoire of the cemetery planter.*

71   *Nunhead cemetery, London, 1863.*

These more bizarre suggestions do not, however, seem to have found such wide acceptance. Although a greater selection of appropriately sombre trees might to some extent provide the cemetery with a distinctive appearance, it remained, on the whole, firmly within the dominant aesthetic of the private or public park. Indeed, Loudon and others suggested that they should to some extent be used like public parks, providing healthy recreation for the public, although of a suitably sombre and educational nature. Loudon was instrumental in promoting the arboreta principle of planting which had such success at Abney Park, Bristol.[57] At the same time, however, he proposed a complicated and

extensive list of rules which were both limiting and exclusive:

No dogs or improper persons; no smoking, drinking, or eating; no running, jumping, laughing, whistling . . .'[58]

Much fine planting can still be seen in urban cemeteries established in the first half of the nineteenth century. Those laid out in the second half of the century, however, seem to be rather less elaborate. From 1852, burial boards were set up and empowered to take over existing cemeteries, and to create new ones.[59] Some of these new burial grounds had a more geometric structure than those created earlier in the century: an engraving of Nunhead in 1863 shows a landscape with elevated rustic flower baskets and a new lime avenue (Fig. 71). But for the most part, late nineteenth-century cemeteries were rather simple and often sparsely-planted affairs, intended simply to provide high-density, low-cost, burial plots for the poorer members of the population. The same was true of additions made to existing cemeteries, and it is significant that larger monuments and mausolea continued to secure prime sites within the original area, long after the extensions were in use. The most famous of English nineteenth-century garden cemeteries, Highgate, was designed by Stephen Geary and opened in 1839. The 8 ha (19 acre) eastern extension was completed shortly after Geary's death in 1854. Important monuments like those to Sir Roland Hill (1878) and Charles Dicken's wife (1879) continued to be erected in the older, more elaborate area of the cemetery; the two largest mausolea, that of the Beer family (built 1876) and Henry William

72   *The Circle of Lebanon, Highgate cemetery, c.1890.*

Eaton's (erected after 1887), were also constructed here on the prestigious Circle of Lebanon, a major feature of the original design (Fig. 72). Perhaps significantly, and certainly symbolically, Karl Marx (1883) was buried in the newer eastern extension.[60]

8 Parks and gardens since 1870

This book has, for the most part, been concerned with the designed landscapes laid out around country houses. The emphasis is intentional for it is these gardens that have made, and still make, the greatest contribution to the present-day English landscape.

Great gardens and parks were for enjoyment and recreation, but they were also status symbols, and instruments of political power. Their creation and maintenance depended upon a certain kind of social and economic system, and this system, already threatened during the middle years of the nineteenth century, came under ever-increasing pressure in the decades after 1870.

The late nineteenth century saw the onset of a serious agricultural depression, caused by competition from new agricultural producers in the New World and elsewhere. In addition, this period saw the culmination of important social and political changes which threatened the pre-eminent position of the traditional landed classes. The landscapes that displayed their power, therefore, gradually lost their *raison d'être*, and this in turn affected the attitudes of those whose wealth was generated in commerce and industry. For such people, the country house, with its elaborate gardens and extensive park, no longer seemed the quintessential symbol of status, but instead it was viewed as an expensive encumbrance.

1880–1914

As the agricultural depression deepened, farms could not be let, rents fell and many large estates grew increasingly impoverished. The problems experienced by landed estates, their retrenchment and, in many cases, their decline have been well documented elsewhere.[1] But such studies have tended to mask the distinction between the wider estate, and the smaller area of designed landscape around the house. Even though the former was in decline, the latter could still be important in the early years of the twentieth century. For although retrenchment was increasingly in the air, change to the grounds of the country house came only gradually. Many ancient families, and those not so ancient, clung on to their gardens and parks, and the exclusivity and seclusion they provided, for as long as economically possible.

Parks, in particular, survived reasonably well in the late nineteenth century. They required little maintenance, and with agriculture in a state of recession there was little incentive to plough them up. A few entirely new parks were even created, although these were mainly laid out for shooting, a sport made fashionable by the passion of the Prince of Wales, and a form of extensive land-use especially suitable for marginal land where farming was now uneconomic. Ken Hill in Norfolk was laid out for the Halifax industrialist Edward

73 *Trentham (Staffordshire): the main parterre and the view towards the lake in 1890. The 'S' motif refers to the family name of Sutherland.*

Green in 1877.[2] It was a far cry from the parks of Brown or Repton. The emphasis was on woodland rides, plantations and coverts for game, rather than on open areas of grassland scattered with trees.

For the most part, however, owners simply reduced expenditure and waited for better times. But society was changing around them, and with it ideas about the landscapes created by the old order. *Gardens Old and New*, a Country Life publication of 1898, reveals some interesting attitudes. Victorian gardens, with their complicated parterres and lengthy avenues, were described as pretentious[3] (Fig. 73). Gardens like Panshanger (Hertfordshire), highly formal and with the family arms laid out in box, had 'great stateliness'[4] but the author's sympathies (and presumably those of some,

at least, of his readers) lay with 'the dear charm of the old domestic garden'.[5] The owners of Ashridge (Hertfordshire), a vast landscape laid out by Brown, Repton and others, had already seen the light: 'the Earl and Countess Brownlow are both interested in the charms of the garden, the arts of the home and the things that are the beauty of country life'.[6] Great designed landscapes were no longer relevant, or sustainable. The power they were intended to display was increasingly empty.

Styles for new times

The special position of the countryside in English society did not disappear with the agricultural depression. If anything, it intensified, and the 'house in the country' continued to have a cultural importance, even if the 'country house' in the traditional sense – with its estate, parkland and elaborate gardens – ceased to be a prerequisite of power.

As in earlier periods, the industrial town was seen as new and ugly, the countryside as old and beautiful; the town as sophisticated and evil, the country as simple and virtuous. 'As we desert the lanes of nature for the cities of artificiality we desert quietude, happiness and integrity for bustle, unrest and insincerity'.[7] In 1898 Barlborough Hall, Chesterfield (Derbyshire) was described as under siege;

the utilitarian needs of the coal fields have shadowed the district with features the reverse of beautiful and the pits that are in the vicinity of this ancient place and the wretched habitations that are their accompaniment have blotted a fair page of nature's book. It is as if the hand of the twentieth century were about to knock on the long-closed gate of the sixteenth, and long may its intrusion by the stout warder be repelled.[8]

Overcrowding, poor sanitation, disease and pollution in towns helped to give the countryside the rosy glow of utopia. But there was more to it than that. Traditionally, England had been ruled by a rurally-based elite, and the close connection between elite status and rural living did not change even as that elite lost much of its power and wealth. Country living was, in itself, a sign of status and success.

So the rich and succesful continued to move out of the city into the country, and, ever outwards beyond the expanding suburbia, country houses with extensive gardens were still being created in the late nineteenth century. Indeed, the fall in land prices made their creation even more viable. In 1878 Joseph Chamberlain established an estate at Highbury, Birmingham. By 1903 the landscaped grounds, in *ferme orneé* tradition, extended over more than 40ha

(100 acres), and included an ornamental dairy, circuit walks, Dutch and Italian Gardens, a tea garden, an Elizabethan garden and no less than 14 hothouses, amongst them one housing Chamberlain's vast orchid collection.[9] In a similar way, the gardens at Aldenham (Hertfordshire) increased in size in the late nineteenth century, again acquiring an ornamental dairy and home farm. The improvements in 1889/90 even involved the removal of a road, in order to increase the size of the area Vicary Gibbs devoted to his horticultural pursuits. Like Highbury, the landscape owed an enormous amount to its owner's passion for planting.[10]

74 *A 'Cottage Garden', as shown in* Gardening Illustrated, *1885.*

75 *An architectural garden. Moor Close, Binfield (Hertfordshire), designed by Oliver Hill.*

These large gardens were fairly exceptional. For most people, the ideal was now to buy up a small country manor house (or something approaching it) and create new gardens around it, in keeping with the imagined simplicity of its former inhabitants. *Gardening Illustrated* in 1885 carried an illustration of a cottage garden (Fig. 74), 'one of the old-fashioned kind' which, it remarked,

is far more pleasing than many more pretentious gardens and there is a charm in the irregular crowded order which may be sought in vain in the prim parterre.[11]

It was simplicity not grandeur, informality not pomp which were the driving ethics behind the new view of the garden.

The earlier nineteenth century garden was, as we have seen, a veritable anarchy of styles. Even individual designers, faced with a wide range of commissions from an increasingly well-informed and exacting public, had difficulty developing personal design idioms, and the resulting chaotic jumble often swarmed uneasily about the walls of the house. The new circumstances of the late nineteenth century changed all this and, in particular, provided great opportunities for the architectural profession. Architects, growing in importance and confidence, had long argued

76 *Hestercombe (Somerset): the garden designed by Gertrude Jekyll and Edwin Lutyens. The house is now the headquarters of the county fire department.*

that the house and garden should be intimately connected, and that the structure of the latter should reflect that of the former. The increasing popularity of the small house in the country now provided further opportunities for putting such notions into practice. The dominance of hard landscaping in many gardens of this period betrays the primary profession of their designers: for instance, Great Tangley Manor (Surrey), 1884 by Philip Webb; Athelhampton Hall (Dorset), 1890 by Inigo Thomas; Hestercombe (Somerset), 1903 by Edwin Lutyens and Gertrude Jekyll; Moor Close, Binfield (Hertfordshire), *c.*1914 by Oliver Hill (Fig. 75).

Without parks or large tracts of farmland, the garden was the key, indeed often the only, designed landscape around the house. The absence of a wider estate landscape ensured that many were now enclosed by walls or hedges, to ensure the privacy of their owners as much as to echo the gardens of the past. The Old Place at Lindfield

(Sussex), was considered beautiful in 1898, partly because it was 'well fenced in from the outside world'.[12] Gardens were, moreover, often partitioned internally, in order to provide a series of compartments which could be used for a variety of healthy games and countrified pursuits, besides gardening.

Such outdoor rooms would have appeared stark without the softening effects of the planting. Architects, used to dealing in straight lines and static forms, were not at ease with the individual and transient nature of plants, and the most successful and influential designs of this period were the product of partnerships between architects and plantspeople. That of Edwin Lutyens and Gertrude Jekyll is the most famous. Their gardens combined a strong sense of order and structure with an air of informality, and created a sense of space by using broad terraces, sweeping steps at changes of level, *clair voyées*, reflective water features and open pergolas and balustrading (Fig. 76). Jekyll had, moreover, one overwhelming advantage over most contemporary designers and owners: the appreciation of colour and tone as it could be applied to planting. It was the painter's eye which produced such works of art as the pink, silver and blue terrace borders in the Deanery Garden and the Spring garden at Munstead Wood (Surrey).

Some owners went to professional plantspeople for advice on what species to use and how to use them (Gertrude Jekyll advised on many gardens), but usually the owner acted as plantsman or woman to the architect. Although later garden writers have tried to detect the hand of the famous partners at gardens such as Sissinghurst,[13] there seems little doubt that most were personal creations. Gardening – as one of the rural, 'natural' pursuits – had a cultural significance among the intelligentsia perhaps greater than ever before. As Walter Wright wrote in *The Perfect Garden* in 1911,

'Cultured people talk of gardening as they talk of books and painting . . . a knowledge of gardening is a part of education'.[14]

The decline in enthusiasm for grand formality in this period, and the economic problems of maintaining large elaborate gardens, produced other kinds of design. In 1870 William Robinson published the first edition of *The Wild Garden*, a popular work which promoted the idea that hardy plants (either native or naturalized) should be allowed to dominate the garden. Robinson insisted that these should not be confined to formal beds but should be distributed in irregular fashion throughout lawns, shrubberies and woodland belts. It is significant that although Robinson wrote 17 books, and many articles, between 1868 and his death in 1935, it is for this work, and for *The English Flower Garden* of 1883, that he is best remembered. The ideas he expounded in these publications were influential because they met the mood of the times. Bulbs naturalized in grass are still a feature of our gardens and orchards (Fig. 77), and although the dream of planting hardy plants which would 'flourish without further care'[15] was difficult to realize in practice, such schemes were certainly less expensive to maintain than earlier styles of gardening.

In keeping with the times, both Robinson and Jekyll placed emphasis on 'old-fashioned flowers'. Robinson was particularly scathing about the use of complicated Latin names, which he associated with exotic introductions and new-fangled varieties. If a suitable colloquial name for a plant did not exist Robinson was not above inventing one (such as Spiked button Snake-Root); it must have caused considerable confusion, and we still bear the legacy of some of these inventions.[16] Wild flowers, too, were introduced into parts of the landscape, particularly into small areas of woodland, although there were reservations voiced even then about the desirability of stripping the countryside of primroses. There was

77 *Cricket St Thomas (Somerset): bulbs naturalized in grass.*

also, significantly, a reinstatement of the term 'meadow'; on small properties this was now considered a more acceptable term than 'park' or 'lawn'.

The decline and revival of the country house landscape

In spite of economic difficulties, many long-established country estates managed to keep up appearances until after the First World War. Often they retained a full gardening staff, and maintained their labour-intensive Victorian gardens. In part, this reflected the deep attachment that families felt to the landscapes of their ancestors. But we should

also remember that many country houses came to be owned by industrial millionaires whose wealth was generated from non-agricultural sources, and who had a particular desire to keep up the appearance of traditional grandeur.

Nevertheless, the upkeep of large-scale, elaborate landscapes was increasingly difficult in the post-war years, and agricultural fortunes, after a brief recovery during the war, returned once more to the doldrums. The sale of landed estates, which had already been increasing in the pre-war years, reached fever-pitch between 1918 and 1922: as much as 25 per cent of England is said to have changed hands in this period, a level of activity in the land market which had not been seen since the Dissolution of the Monasteries. Many estates were in a poor condition when sold and the purchasers often demolished the mansion and converted the park to other uses. The Forestry Commission was a major purchaser of country estates, especially of those on marginal land, and the report prepared when Croxton (Norfolk), was aquired in 1923 describes a not untypical scene of dereliction:

The various land and timber speculators through which these lands have passed during the past 7 years are responsible for the deplorable condition of the estate . . . In consequence of the timber operations the park, as such, has ceased to exist. An avenue of limes and a few quasi-ornamental trees of little commercial value are all that are left, except in a few wild belts where a few ragged conifers remain, the best timber having been cut out.[17]

What remained of the park was obliterated by conifer plantations, a fate experienced by a number of other parks, especially in eastern England, during this period. But other landscapes lost at this time have left more tangible traces. Where parks were turned over to agriculture, for example, the perimeter belts often survive still today, even if the clumps and free-standing timber have fallen to the plough.

In the vicinity of major towns and cities, parks often provided suitable areas for suburban development, public parks or golf courses. Cassiobury Park (Hertfordshire) was sold off in a number of stages in the 1920s, and different parts of the park were converted to all these uses. The development potential of one of the largest plots offered in the sale of 1922 was described in glowing terms:

Its contiguity to the important town of Watford with its growing population . . . coupled with the fact that there are no less than 7,700 feet of available frontages to existing roads, constitutes the Estate one of the Finest Buildings Propositions within this distance of London . . . while the Mansion itself, apart from its Residential attractions, might readily be converted into an Hotel, Public Institution, or Convalescent Home.[18]

In the event, this house was demolished, although conversion to institutional use was becoming increasingly common in this period. Within the area of the park converted to a middle-class housing estate all trace of the former landscape has been obliterated, but in the portion converted to golf course and public park much of the early planting, including the magnificent early eighteenth-century lime avenue, still survives.

Most country house landscapes survived reasonably intact in the inter-war period, although resources were reduced, and this frequently had a profound effect on the gardens. Luxuries such as great glasshouses and hot houses were dispensed with: the Great Stove at Chatsworth was one of many demolished in the early 1920s. Staff levels were cut, and the layout of parterres and flower beds systematically simplified. Sometimes owners made a virtue of necessity, as at Blickling (Norfolk), where the complicated Victorian parterre was modified to a less formal design created by Norah Lindsay, one of Gertrude Jekyll's disciples.

The Second World War marked another watershed. Country house gardens were frequently maintained by only the one or two members of the estate staff who were too old for conscription. The 'Dig for Victory' campaign changed the face of many parks, although the meagre results often confirmed the low arable productivity of the land which, for historic reasons, they often occupied.[19] Even gardens near the house might be forced into production, as at Chatsworth.[20] A few were deliberately removed: the intricate parterre at

Somerleyton (Suffolk) was grassed over because it was felt that its white gravel would provide a landmark for enemy bombers.[21] Only a handful of country houses were actually bombed (Trafford Park, Manchester; Sandling Park, Kent etc.) but many were commandeered for use by the army, schools or institutions, something which often had a disastrous effect on the landscape. Concrete roads, trenches and bunkers dotted parks; many, especially in the south and east of England, still bear the archaeological traces of this phase of their development (Fig. 78).

Country house landscapes continued to deteriorate in the post-War years. Compensation for damage, or for lack of maintenance, caused by wartime use was almost universally considered inadequate; at Aldenham (Hertfordshire) in 1948 £11,000

was awarded, against the £21,700 claimed.[22] The owner of Ditchley Park (Oxfordshire), redesigned by Geoffrey Jellicoe in the 1930s, finally abandoned it in frustration when he was refused a permit for the erection of entrance gates, because of the post-war shortages.[23] Even when agricultural fortunes began to recover during, and after, the war, the fortunes of the country house did not necessarily improve. Many were converted to new uses, as research establishments, schools or hotels. The houses might thus survive, but the gardens were frequently allowed to deteriorate, while the parkland was sold off for other uses: agriculture, mineral extraction or housing. Even where the house remained in private ownership, the park was frequently sacrificed, and ornamental estate buildings, many rendered redundant by the lack of staff

78   *The remains of Haveringland Park (Norfolk), commandeered by the army during the Second World War. The hall is now demolished and the park has reverted to farmland.*

79 *Chipping Campden (Gloucestershire): the East Banqueting House, Restored by The Landmark Trust and now used as a holiday home.*

to inhabit them, were allowed to fall into disrepair and were eventually demolished.

A revival came for many in the more affluent times of the late 1950s and 1960s. Since 1937 the National Trust had been assuming responsibility for many of these large white elephants: such acquisitions, and the initiatives of private owners, now led to country houses being opened to the public on a scale never seen before. Increasing mobility among the middle class provided the market, and today, while most would not spend their bank holidays in the local city park they are quite content with a trip to Sissinghurst or Stourhead. More recently,

ornamental garden and estate buildings, instead of being demolished, have become prime targets for conversion to holiday homes. The 1991 brochure for one of main letting agencies for holiday cottages included over a hundred former estate buildings ranging from gamekeepers' and coachmens' cottages to gate-lodges and gardeners' bothies.[24] The Landmark Trust's 1991 list had even more exotic conversions: the former Bath House to Walton Hall (Warwickshire); a pig-sty built as a Greek temple at Fyling Hall (Yorkshire); and the East Banqueting House at Chipping Camden, Gloucestershire (Fig. 79).[25]

Today, parks and gardens not only cater for the nation's fascination with the past; some have diversified in ways reminiscent of the early eighteenth-century pleasure garden, their landscapes disintegrating into theme parks, as at Alton Towers (Staffordshire) (although here the garden remains surprisingly intact and under-visited), while Blenheim and Chatsworth vie with each other in the provision of adventure playgrounds, mazes and pitch-and-put; and Longleat has its lions. But the market will only take so many tourist honey-pots, and less remarkable or extensive landscapes continue to find other functions in the leisure industry, especially as golf courses.

In the 1980s and 1990s, with the development of England as a kind of huge historical theme park, increasing amounts of public money, funnelled in a bewildering variety of ways, have provided a further life-line for landscapes deemed part of the nation's 'heritage'. Indeed, public money can be granted to private landscapes even if they are not regularly opened to the public. It is significant that at a time when the resources of municipal Parks Departments are dwindling, when legislation has forced them to go out to tender for maintenance, and when many public parks have been reduced to little more than bare recreation grounds – increasingly large sums are being expended in grants and subsidies on landscapes in the hands of private families.

Are such landscapes really 'our' heritage, and should public money be poured into their preservation? Even if we answer (as many readers probably would) with a resounding 'yes', we are nevertheless faced with a whole range of very difficult practical and philosophical questions. Not only are most of these landscapes well past their prime, their whole purpose, and function, has radically changed. When a park is restored, what particular period should it be restored to? Most are complex, multi-period

artefacts, and returning a landscape to the way it was in, say, 1800 would usually involve the destruction of formal gardens and other features added in the nineteenth century. Should these landscapes simply be maintained in their present state of development, replanting features of all periods as they grow old and die? This is not always an easy matter, for practical horticultural reasons – especially when it comes to replacing fallen trees in clumps or avenues, right next to mature specimens. What is to be done about accommodating the facilities necessary for opening these places to the public – the toilets, car-parks, cafeterias and wheel-chair access ways and the rest? And what about new aesthetic additions to these landscapes: should they be encouraged (there is no way, in the present state of conservation legislation, that they can be stopped)? Or are parks and gardens to be preserved forever in aspic, as suggested in the term now so widely applied to them: 'historic landscapes', landscapes of the past, sealed, their further development ended?

These are difficult questions, intimately connected with wider debates about conservation and politics. What is beyond debate, however, is that the twentieth century no longer has a clear concept of large-scale landscape design. The Institute of Landscape Architects was established, originally as the British Association of Garden Architects, in December 1929. It is unlikely that the present day commissions of its members are quite what its first president, the 'arts and crafts' designer Thomas Mawson, envisaged. Planning consents for new industrial, institutional or amenity building invariably carry a clause relating to the surrounding landscape. Unfortunately, such schemes are usually funded on what is left from the overall contract and, as the contract proceeds, cash is progressively reduced by overspend on the buildings. Motorway embankments, city centre car-parks, out-of-town shopping centres and slag heap reclamation schemes constitute the largest part of the work of the profession today, work often underfunded and frequently frustrating. 'Minimum maintenance' all too often sounds the death knell on a landscape design. Landscape architects are, by and large, involved in cosmetics, not in art. They rarely have the opportunity to design extensive new landscapes, although they often play a valuable role in the conservation of old ones. For few new private landscapes are now created; and no large-scale landscape aesthetic, modernist or post-modernist, has developed. Perhaps the future will see a new kind of public patron, with a new style: the establishment of the 'people's forests' in redundant industrial land may point the way.[27] But at the moment, large-scale aesthetic landscape designs are a thing of the past.

Smaller gardens

We have said very little in this book about the smaller gardens in the English landscape, because these are the most ephemeral of all. The remains of nineteenth-century suburban villa gardens can still make an important impact on urban and suburban scenery, but for the most part the smaller gardens in the town and countryside, which collectively occupy a considerable acreage, are of relatively recent design. Trees and hedges planted in the early decades of the twentieth century are quite common features, especially the privet and beech hedges which, before the advent of the dreaded *leylandii*, were ubiquitous in the suburban and urban garden.

Some shrub planting also survives from the early part of this century. Detailed survey work is currently being undertaken by the National Council for the Conservation of Plants and Gardens to identify more ephemeral plants which might

have survived by continuous propagation, but the majority of plants in the smaller gardens are of mid- or late twentieth-century date. This is partly because the kinds of plant suitable for most small plots are fairly short-lived. But it is also because the design of gardens tends to change rapidly with the arrival of each new owner. Moreover, while no new style of large-scale landscaping was to emerge in the twentieth century, the design of small gardens in the towns and suburbs continued to develop, in ways which cannot be discussed here. And this, in turn, is a reflection of the fact that gardens, and gardening, retained their central position in English culture throughout the twentieth century.

The Garden City Movement, founded by Ebeneezer Howard, reflects this centrality in its very name. Garden Cities like Letchworth (1903) and Welwyn Garden City (1920) were intended to be self-sufficient units with easy access to work and amenities. Each house had its own garden, generally both back and front, and the wider environment was embellished with street planting, parks and greens. The private speculators responsible for the thousands of acres of suburbs and ribbon-developments which sprawled through the countryside in the inter-war years were unwilling to provide this kind of wider amenity landscape, but the neat rows of semis were, nevertheless, invariably provided with private gardens. The heavy bombing of cities in the Second World War gave the opportunity to create more housing with gardens, and more garden cities, but the incredible scale of the post-war housing problem, the shortage of cash, and the dominance of a modernist architectural clique led to a different solution: the erection of system-built tower blocks and tenements with a communal recreation ground in the windswept areas between.

Curiously, such landscapes are castigated – in a very different social and economic

80 *One of the estate village gardens at Harlaxton (Lincolnshire). Sold off into private ownership, several of these have now been reduced to hard standing.*

climate – at the same time as the small private garden in the towns and cities appears to be experiencing something of a decline. As early as 1937 Ralph Dutton was predicting: '. . . undoubtedly there will be a tendency towards more compact layouts which can be economically worked by a small staff of gardeners'.[26] As most members of the middle class ceased to keep domestic staff, garden layouts were simplified, in spite of the proliferation of an ever-greater range of labour-saving devices. Other forces are at work in the urban landscape. The general increase in car ownership, and the absence of original provision for parking, has led to the obliteration of many front gardens by hard standing (Fig. 80). Many substantial houses have been divided into flats or offices, with a predictable fate for the garden. Many gardens have been divided to provide building plots, as urban and suburban property prices soar.

Yet, England still has thousands of acres of gardens. Even in the cities, gardens are often treasured and much sought after; while in the leafy suburbs and in the countryside, few houses are without their well-tended plot. Gardening is a national obsession, catered for by television programmes, radio, books, magazines, nurseries and garden centres. Perhaps this enthusiasm reflects the increasing lack of control which most people have over the wider environment: we strive to maintain surroundings we know and recognize, in which we feel 'at home' and which are under our personal direction. Perhaps the alienation of modern life encourages the sense of personal achievement which so many derive from gardening. Perhaps the peculiarly English obsession with the private garden is connected with the strong sense of individualism deeply rooted in English culture: each man has his castle, each man his estate. Whatever the explanation, the small private plot with its plant collections, rockeries, wild gardens or even just lawn is cherished with a fervour out of all proportion to its size.

CHESTER COLLEGE LIBRARY

Notes

Chapter 1 (pages 11–29)

1 Norfolk Record Office, Ms 7708 19B4, Haverland Box A; Ms 7705 19B3, Haverland Box A (letters and accounts relating to the purchase of Haveringland, 1777–80).
2 G.H. Whalley, *The Tithe Act and the Tithe Amendment Act*, Shaw & Sons (on behalf of the Tithe Commissioners), London, 1838.
3 J.B. Harley, *Maps for Local Historians*, National Council of Social Service and J.B. Harley, London, 1972, pp.63–76.
4 Humphry Repton, *Fragments on the Theory and Practice of Landscape Gardening*, Bensley & Son, London, 1816, p.106.
5 Norfolk Record Office, BUL 9/134/2.
6 Norfolk Record Office, Hare 5529 223X5.
7 Norfolk Record Office, Hare 5531 223X5.
8 Norfolk Record Office, MC 124/5.
9 There are many good books on the interpretation of earthworks. See, in particular, A.E. Brown, *Fieldwork for Archaeologists and Local Historians*, Batsford, London, 1988; and Christoper Taylor, *Fieldwork in Medieval Archaeology*, Batsford, London, 1974.
10 Timothy Darvill, *Ancient Monuments in the Countryside: an Archaeological Management Review*, Historic Buildings and Monuments Commission, London, 1987, p.138.
11 Christopher Taylor, *The Archaeology of Gardens*, Shire, Aylesbury, 1983.
12 Which is, unquestionably: Alan Mitchell, *A Field Guide to the Trees of Britain and Northern Europe*, Collins, London, 1974, p.25.
13 *Ibid.*
14 Moses Cook, *The Manner of Raising, Ordering and Improving Forest Trees*, London, 1676.
15 C.D. Pigott, 'Estimation of the age of lime trees (*Tilia spp*) in parklands from stem diameter and ring counts', *Arboricultural Journal* 13 (1989), pp.289–302.

Chapter 2 (pages 30–47)

1 Teresa McLean, *Medieval English Gardens*, Collins, London, 1981, p.31.
2 John Harvey, 'The Square Garden of Henry the Poet', *Garden History* 15, 1 (1987), pp.1–11.
3 This account draws heavily on: John Harvey, *Medieval Gardens*, Batsford, London 1981; and McLean, *op.cit.*
4 McLean, *op.cit.*, pp.92–5.
5 *Ibid*, p.102.
6 John Harvey, *Restoring Period Gardens*. Shire, Aylesbury, 1988, pp.21–2.
7 Harvey, *Medieval Gardens*, p.110.
8 Christopher Taylor, *The Archaeology of Gardens*, Shire, Aylesbury, 1983, pp.38–9.
9 *Ibid.*, pp.34–8.
10 James Grieg, 'Plant Resources', in Grenville Astill and Annie Grant (eds) *The Countryside of Medieval England*, Oxford, Blackwell, 1988, pp.102–27, p.114.
11 Grenville Astill, 'Rural Settlement; the Toft and the Croft', in G. Astill and A. Grant, *op.cit.*, pp.36–61, p.47.
12 See, in particular: Oliver Rackham, *The History of the Countryside*, Dent, London, 1986, pp.122–9; and Paul Stamper, 'Woods and Parks', in G. Astill and A. Grant *op.cit.*, pp.128–48.

13 R.T. Rowley, *The Landscape of the Welsh
    Marches*, London, 1986, p.149. Della Hooke,
    Anglo-Saxon Landscapes of the West Midlands.
    British Archaeological Reports British Series
    95, Oxford 1981, pp.54–6.

14 Leonard Cantor, *The Medieval Parks of
    England: A Gazetteer*, Loughborough
    University Press, Loughborough, 1982.

15 Paul Stamper, *op.cit.*, p.141.

16 John Harvey, 'Pleasance', in G. Jellicoe, P.
    Goode, and M. Lancaster (eds) *The Oxford
    Companion to Gardens*, Oxford University
    Press, Oxford, 1986, pp.438–41.

17 *Ibid.*

18 McLean, *op.cit.*, pp.99–101.

19 David Hinton, *Archaeology, Economy, and
    Society: England from the Fifth to the Fifteenth
    Century*, Seaby, London, 1990, p.170.
    Michael Aston (ed.) *Medieval Fish, Fishponds,
    and Fisheries in England*. British
    Archaeological Reports, British Series 182,
    1988, Chapter 7, Note 9.

20 C. Taylor, P. Everson, and R. Wilson-
    North, 'Bodiam Castle, Sussex'. *Medieval
    Archaeology* 34 (1990), pp.155–7.

21 John Harvey, *Restoring Period Gardens*, p.30.

22 Vincent B. Redstone, 'Notes on Suffolk
    Castles'. *Proceedings of the Suffolk Institute of
    Archaeology* 11 (1900), pp.301–19.

23 Christopher Taylor, *op.cit.*, pp.13–25.

24 The best discussions of the Renaissance
    garden in England are: John Dixon Hunt,
    *Garden and Grove: the Italian Renaissance
    Garden in the English Imagination 1600–1750*,
    Dent, London, 1986; and Roy Strong, *The
    Renaissance Garden in England*, Thames and
    Hudson, London, 1979.

25 John Dixon Hunt, *op.cit.*, p.103.

26 Roy Strong, *op.cit.*, pp.50–7.

27 Roy Strong, *op.cit.*, pp.56–7.

28 Royal Commission on Historical
    Monuments, *An Inventory of the Historical
    Monuments in the County of Northampton,
    Volume 3: Archaeological Sites in
    Northamptonshire*, HMSO, London, 1981,
    pp.105–11.

29 Paul Everson, 'The Gardens of Campden
    House, Chipping Campden, Gloucestershire',
    Garden History 17, 2 (1989), pp.109–21.

30 Tom Williamson and Anthea Taigel, 'Some
    Early Geometric Gardens in Norfolk'. *Journal
    of Garden History* 11, 1 and 2 (1991), pp.82–4.

31 Roy Strong, *op.cit.*, pp.147–65.

32 East Suffolk Record Office, 295; East Suffolk
    Record Office, 942.64 Som.

33 A.E. Brown and C. Taylor, 'Cambridgeshire
    Earthwork Surveys II'. *Proceedings of the
    Cambridgeshire Antiquarian Society* 67 (1977),
    pp.85–94; 99–101.

34 See, for example, Tom Turner, *English
    Garden Design: History and Styles Since 1650*,
    Antique Collectors Club, Woodbridge, 1986,
    pp.44–74.

35 Frank Woodward, *Oxfordshire Parks*,
    Oxfordshire Museum Service, Woodstock,
    1982.

36 Tom Williamson and Anthea Taigel *op.cit.*,
    pp.89–90.

37 *Ibid.*, pp.85–8.

38 Berkshire Record Office, D/ED F 14.

39 For good discussions of garden earthworks,
    see Brown and Taylor, *op.cit*; Taylor, *op.cit.*;
    and Michael Aston, 'Gardens and
    Earthworks at Hardingham and Low Ham',
    Somerset Archaeology and Natural History 122
    (1978), pp.11–18.

Chapter 3 (pages 48–64)

1 Miles Hadfield, *A History of British Gardening*,
   London, 1960, pp.179–240. John Dixon
   Hunt and Peter Willis, *The Genius of the Place*,
   London, 1975, pp.1–43. Christopher
   Hussey, *English Gardens and Landscapes 1700–
   1750*, London, 1967. More recent work has
   presented a more complex picture. See, in
   particular, David Jaques' *Georgian Gardens:
   the Reign of Nature*, Batsford, London, 1983.

2 B. Hill, *The Growth of Parliamentary Parties,
   1689–1742*, Allen and Unwin, London, 1976.
   B. Hill, *Sir Robert Walpole*, Hamilton,
   London, 1989. J.C.D. Clark, *English Society
   1688–1832: Ideology, Social Structure, and
   Political Practice During the Ancien Regime*,
   Cambridge University Press, 1985.

3 J.C.D. Clark, *Revolution and Rebellion: State
   and Society in England in the Seventeenth and
   Eighteenth Centuries*, Cambridge University
   Press, 1986.

4 The Diary of Hamon Le Strange, 1705–1712. Norfolk Record Office, Le Strange NF 2.

5 Charles Perry's Tour of Northern England. Norfolk Record Office, MC 150/49.

6 Tom Williamson and Anthea Taigel, 'Some Early Geometric Gardens in Norfolk', *Journal of Garden History* 11, 1 and 2 (1991), pp.86–7.

7 Batty Langley, *Practical Geometry Applied to the Useful Arts of Building, Surveying, and Gardening*, London, 1729, p.38.

8 Tom Williamson and Liz Bellamy, *Property and Landscape: a Social History of Landownership and the English Countryside*, George Philip, London, 1987, pp.141–3. Hugh Prince, *Parks in England*. Isle of Wight, 1967. Leonard Cantor, *The Changing English Countryside 1400–1700*, Routledge and Kegan Paul, London, 1987, pp.113–14.

9 E.P. Thompson, *Whigs and Hunters: the Origin of the Black Act*, Allen Lane, London, 1975.

10 Dan Cruickshank, *A Guide to the Georgian Buildings of Britain and Ireland*, Weidenfeld and Nicolson for the National Trust, London, 1985, pp.2–23.

11 C.M. Sicca, 'Lord Bathurst at Chiswick; Architecture and Landscape', *Garden History* 10, 1 (1982), pp.36–69. J. Carree, 'Lord Burlington's Garden at Chiswick', *Garden History* 1, 3 (1973), pp.23–30.

12 Robin Fausset, 'The Creation of the Gardens at Castle Hill, South Molton, Devon', *Garden History* 13, 2 (1985), pp.102–25.

13 Stephen Switzer, *Ichnographia Rustica, Volume 1*. London, 1718, p.34.

14 Berkshire Record Office, D/EX 258/9.

15 Tom Williamson and Anthea Taigel *op.cit.*, pp.59–65.

16 Christopher Taylor, *The Archaeology of Gardens*, Shire, Aylesbury, 1983, pp.55–6.

17 *Ibid.*, pp.60–1.

18 M.R. Brownell, 'The Garden of Horatio and Pope's Twickenham: an Unnoticed Parallel', *Garden History* 5, 2 (1977), pp.9–24. A.J. Sambrook, 'The Shape and Size of Pope's Garden', *Eighteenth-Century Studies* 5 (1977), pp.450–5. David Jaques, 'The Art and Sense of the Scriblerus Club in England, 1715–1735', *Garden History* 4, 1 (1976), pp.30–53.

19 Alexander Pope, *Poetical Works*, Edited by Herbert Davis. Oxford University Press, 1966, p.318.

20 Jaques, *op.cit.*, 35.

21 *The Spectator*, No. 44, 25 June 1712.

22 Switzer, *op.cit.*

23 *Ibid.*, pp.34–7.

24 Historic Manuscripts Commission Report 42, *Carlisle*, pp.143–4.

25 George Clarke, 'Grecian Taste and Gothic Virtue: Lord Cobham's Gardening Programme and its Iconography', *Apollo* 97 (1973), pp.56–67.

26 Kimerley Rorschach, *The Early Georgian Landscape Garden*, New Haven, Connecticut, 1983, pp.39–45.

27 Paul Edwards, 'The gardens at Wroxton Abbey, Oxfordshire', *Garden History* 14, 1 (1986), pp.50–9.

28 Alison Hodges, 'Painshill Park, Cobham, Surrey 1700–1800', *Garden History* 2, 2 (1973), pp.39–68. Michael Symes, 'Charles Hamilton's Plantings at Painshill', *Garden History* 11, 2 (1983), pp.112–24.

29 Mavis Batey, 'The Way to View Rousham by Kent's Gardener', *Garden History* 11, 2 (1983), pp.125–32. For information about Rousham see, in particular, Hal Moggridge, 'Notes on Kent's Garden at Rousham', *Journal of Garden History* 6, 3 (1986), pp.187–226.

30 Information derived from John Harvey, *Restoring Period Gardens*, Shire, Aylesbury, 1988, pp.78–99.

31 Mavis Batey, *op.cit.*; Simon Pugh, *Garden-Nature-Language*, Manchester University Press 1988, pp.46–76.

32 R.W. King, 'Phillip Southcote and Woburn Farm', *Garden History* 2, 3 (1974), pp.27–60.

33 Kimerley Rorschach, *op.cit.*, pp.39–45.

34 *The World*, No. 15, 12 April 1753.

35 Berkshire Record Office, D/ELL Cl/240.

36 Drury and Andrews *Map of the County of Hertford*. Published 1766. Cambridgeshire University Library.

37 Hertfordshire Record Office, D/EB 1622 P3.

38 See, for example, John Harris, 'Gardenesque: the Case of Charles Grevile's Garden at Gloucester', *Journal of Garden History* 1, 1 (1981), pp.167–78.

Chapter 4 (pages 65–81)

1   Miles Hadfield, *A History of British Gardening*, London, 1960, pp.179–240.

2   John Dixon Hunt and Peter Willis, *The Genius of the Place*, London, 1975, pp.1–43. Christopher Hussey, *English Gardens and Landscapes 1700–1750*. London, 1967.

3   Dorothy Stroud, *Capability Brown*, Country Life, London, 1965. Roger Turner, *Capability Brown and the Eighteenth-Century English Landscape*, Weidenfeld and Nicolson, London, 1985. Thomas Hinde, *Capability Brown: the Story of a Master Gardener*, Hutchinson, London, 1986.

4   Oliver Rackham, *The History of the Countryside*, Dent, London, 1986, pp.128–9. Oliver Rackham, *Trees and Woodlands in the British Landscape*, Dent, London, pp.148–9. Tom Williamson and Liz Bellamy, *Property and Landscape: a Social History of Land Ownership and the English Countryside*, George Philip, London, 1987, pp.144–50. Bryan E. Coates, 'Parkland in Transition: Medieval Deer Park to Modern Landscape Park', *Transactions of the Hunter Archaeological Society* 9 (1969), pp.132–41.

5   Tom Williamson and Anthea Taigel, 'Some Early Geometric gardens in Norfolk', *Journal of Garden History* 11, 1 and 2 (1991), p.10.

6   Fiona Cowell, 'Richard Woods (?1716–93). A Preliminary Account, Part 1', *Garden History* 14, 2 (1986), pp.85–120. Fiona Cowell, 'Richard Woods (?1716–93). A Preliminary Account, Part 2', *Garden History* 15, 1 (1987), pp.19–54. Fiona Cowell, 'Richard Woods (?1716–93). A Preliminary Account, Part 3', *Garden History* 15, 2 (1987), pp.115–35.

7   Humphry Repton, *Fragments on the Theory and Practice of Landscape Gardening*, Bensley and Son, London, 1816.

8   Dorothy Stroud, *op.cit.*, pp.68–9.

9   Buckinghamshire Record Office.

10 David Jaques, *Georgian Gardens: the Reign of Nature*, Batsford, London, 1983, p.72 and Plate IV. Hugh Bilbrough, 'Documents in Record Offices which might affect the assessment of the achievement of "Capability" Brown', *Garden History* 1, 3 (1973), pp.9–22.

11 Figure 36 is based on William Faden's map of Norfolk, 1797; Joseph Hodskinson's map of Suffolk, 1783; and J. Stockdales' map of Essex, 1797. For developments in another area, see Sue Farrant, 'The Development of Landscape Parks and Gardens in Eastern Sussex *c.*1700 to 1820 – A Guide and Gazetteer', *Garden History* 17, 2 (1989), pp.166–180.

12 Neil McKendrick, John Brewer, John Plumb, *The Birth of a Consumer Society*, Europa, London, 1982.

13 Mark Girouard, *English Towns*, Yale University Press, London and New Haven, 1990, pp.76–9.

14 Tom Williamson and Liz Bellamy, *Property and Landscape*, George Philip, London, 1987, pp.94–115. J.A. Yelling, *Common Field and Enclosure*, London, 1977. M.E. Turner, *English Parliamentary Enclosure*, Folkestone, 1980. Keith Snell, *Annals of the Labouring Poor: Social Change and Agrarian England 1660–1900*, Cambridge University Press, 1983.

15 Oliver Goldsmith, *The Traveller*, lines 405–410.

16 Williamson and Bellamy *op.cit.*, pp.136–9.

17 Christopher Taylor, *Village and Farmstead: A History of Rural Settlement in England*, George Philip, London, 1983, p.211.

18 M.F. Hughes, 'Emparking and the Desertion of Settlements in Hampshire', *Medieval Village Research Group Report* 30 (1982), p.37.

19 B.A. Holderness, '"Open" and "Close" Parishes in England in the Eighteenth and Nineteenth Centuries', *Agricultural History Review* 20 (1972), pp.126–39. D.R. Mills, *Lord and Peasant in Nineteenth-Century Britain*, London, 1980.

20 Augustus Jessop (ed.), *The Autobiography of the Hon. Roger North*, London, 1887, p.199.

21 Tom Williamson and Anthea Taigel, 'Some Early Geometric Gardens in Norfolk', *Journal of Garden History* 11, 1 and 2 (1991), pp.59–65.

22 Norfolk Record Office, Road Order Book 3, 290–2.

23 Humphry Repton, *Red Book for Tewin*, Hertfordshire Record Office, D/Z 42 Z1 P 21A.

24 Dorothy Stroud *op.cit.*, p.234; 243.

25 Tom Williamson and Anthea Taigel, *op.cit.*, pp.34–7.

26 Norfolk Record Office, HEA 489 256X4.

27 Hertfordshire Record Office, A 2845.

28 Henry Home, Lord Kames, *Elements of Criticism*, London, 1762, p.85.

29 K.M. Goodway, 'William Emes', in G. Jellicoe, P. Goode, and M. Lancaster (eds) *The Oxford Companion to Gardens*, Oxford University Press, Oxford, 1986, p.161.

30 David Jaques, *op.cit.*, pp.95–101.

31 Sir Uvedale Price, *Essay on the Picturesque, as Compared With the Sublime and the Beautiful, and on the Use of Studying Pictures for the Purpose of Improving Landscape*, three volumes, Robson, London, 1796–1798. Richard Payne Knight, *The Landscape: a Didactic Poem in 3 Books*, Nicol, London, 1795.

32 Jay Appleton, 'Some Thoughts on the Geography of the Picturesque', *Journal of Garden History* 6, 3 (1986), pp.270–91.

33 John Britton, *A History and Description of Cassiobury Park in Hertfordshire*, London, 1837.

34 Dorothy Stroud, *Humphry Repton*, Country Life, London, 1962. George Carter, Patrick Goode and Kedrun Laurie (eds) *Humphry Repton, Landscape Gardener, 1752–1818*, Sainsbury Centre, Norwich, 1982.

35 Steve Daniels, 'The Political Landscape', in George Carter, Patrick Goode, and Kedrun Laurie *op.cit.*, pp.110–21.

36 J.C. Loudon, *The Landscape Gardening and Landscape Architecture of the Late Humphry Repton*, London, 1840, p.92.

Chapter 5 (pages 82–103)

1 T.H.D. Turner, 'John Claudius Loudon', in G. Jellicoe, P. Goode, and M. Lancaster (eds) *The Oxford Companion to Gardens*, Oxford University Press, Oxford, 1986, pp.344.

2 J.C. Loudon, *Remarks on Certain Improvements Proposed to be Executed at Gillingham Hall*, Ms, private collection, 1812.

3 *The Gardener's Magazine*, 1829, p.687.

4 J.C. Loudon, *The Suburban Gardener and Villa Companion*, London, 1838.

5 Miles Hadfield, *A History of British Gardening*, Penguin Books, Harmondsworth, 1960, p.308.

6 *Ibid.*, p.311.

7 Brent Elliott, *Victorian Gardens*, Batsford, London, 1986, pp.71–4. Lawrence Fleming and Alan Gore, *The English Garden*, Michael Joseph, London, 1979, p.190. Miles Hadfield, *op.cit.*, p.308.

8 George Chadwick, *The Works of Sir Joseph Paxton*, The Architectural Press, London, 1961.

9 *Norfolk Chronicle*, 4 October, 1800.

10 For example, *Gardener's Chronicle*, 1862, p.928, advertisement by William Short.

11 J.C. Loudon, *A Treatise on Forming, Improving and Managing Country Residences*, Longmans, London, 1806, Vol. 2, p.491.

12 Benjamin Samuel Williams, *Choice Stove, Greenhouse, and Ornamental Leaved Plants*, London, 1876.

13 Edward Kemp, *How to Lay out a Garden*, Bradbury and Evans, London, 1864, p.31.

14 *Gardening Illustrated for Town and Country*, 1885, p.532.

15 The parterre laid out at Castle Ashby in the 1860s, for example, bore the family arms of the Northampton family.

16 Baron Ferdinand de Rothschild at Mentmore, Buckinghamshire, in the 1870s. Lawrence Fleming and Alan Gore, *The English Garden*, Michael Joseph, London, 1979, p.240.

17 Edward Kemp, *op.cit.*, p.36.

18 *Paxton's Magazine of Botany*, 1834, p.211.

19 Edward Kemp, *op.cit.*, p.4.

20 Augustus Jessop, *Arcady: For Better, For Worse*, Fisher and Unwin, London, 1887, p.10.

21 Martin Wainwright in *Country Times and Landscapes*, Evro, London, 1988.

22 Edward Kemp, *op.cit.*, p.186.

23 *Ibid.*, p.240.

24 Humphry Repton, *Fragments on the Theory and Practice of Landscape Gardening*, Bensley & Son, London, 1816, p.36.

25 *Ibid.*, p.206.

26 Anthony J. Lambert, *Victorian and Edwardian Country House Life From Old Photographs*, Batsford, London, 1981, p.8.

27 Edward Kemp, *op.cit.*, p.359.

28 Andrew Clayton-Payne and Brent Elliott, *Victorian Flower Gardens*, Weidenfeld and Nicolson, London, 1988, p.46.

29 Edward Kemp, *op.cit.*, p.359.

30 Princess Fryderyk Wilhelm Antoni Radziwill, *Memoirs of the Duchess de Dino*, Volume 1. London, 1909, pp.56–7.

31 Edward Kemp, *op.cit.*, p.236.

32 Tim Warner, 'Early landscape preservation'. *The East Midland Geographer* 12, 1 and 2 (1989), pp.34–43.

33 *Ibid.*

34 *The Dalesman*, 44, 5 (1982), p.373.

35 George Chadwick, *op.cit.*, p.242.

36 Lionel Munby, *The Hertfordshire Landscape*, Hodder and Stoughton, London, 1977, pp.212–19.

37 *Proceedings of the Horticultural Society of London* 1851/2, p.173.

38 *Curtis's Botanical Magazine* 10, Third Series, 1854, 4777 and 4778.

39 *Proceedings of the Horticultural Society of London*, 1860, pp.596–608.

40 Alistair Forsyth, *Yesterday's Gardens*, Royal Commission on Historic Monuments, London, 1983, illustration 44.

41 Brent Elliott, *op.cit.*, pp.117–18.

42 *Ibid.*, p.84.

43 *The Gardener's Magazine* 11 (1835), p.385.

44 Alexander Forsyth, 'Game Preserves and Fences', *Journal of the Horticultural Society* 1 (1846), p.201.

45 Brent Elliott, *op.cit.*, pp.77–8.

46 'Bicton', English Heritage, *Register of Parks and Gardens of Special Historic Interest in England. Part 2: Devon*. London, n.d.

47 Devon County Record Office, Rolle Mss. 96M Box 30/9. Bicton Estates, 1875–80.

48 Humphry Repton, *Fragments on the Theory and Practice of Landscape Gardening*, Bensley and Son, London, 1816, p.137.

Chapter 6 (pages 104–18)

1 Colonel Wilford, *A Short Treatise on Pasture Land fences: their Culture, Management, and Restoration*, London, 1862, pp.18–19.

2 Humphry Repton, *Fragments on the Theory and Practice of Landscape Gardening*, Bensley & Son, London, 1816, p.45.

3 Jean Holt (ed.), *The Staniforth Diary: a Visit to Cornwall in 1800*, Warne, St Austell, 1965. Entries for 29 August and 8 September.

4 Norfolk Record Office, WCK 407 X 6.

5 *Ibid.*

6 Norfolk Record Office, MC 77/1.

7 Norfolk Record Office, MC 3/284.

8 Humphry Repton *op.cit.*, p.175.

9 Alexander Forsyth, 'Game Preserves and Fences', *Journal of the Horticultural Society* 1 (1846), p.201. For an important discussion of the role of hunting in the landscape park, see the seminal article by Robert Williams, 'Rural Economy and the Antique in the English Landscape Garden', *Journal of Garden History* 7, 1 (1987), pp.73–96.

10 Susan Seymour, 'The Spirit of Planting', *The East Midlands Geographer* 12, 1 and 2 (1989), pp.5–13.

11 W. Adam. *Gem of the Peak*, John & Charles Mozley, Derby, 1857. For general information on the kitchen garden see, in particular, Susan Campbell, 'The Genesis of Queen Victoria's Great New Kitchen Garden', *Garden History* 12, 2 (1984), pp.100–19; Jennifer Davies. *The Victorian Kitchen Garden*, BBC Books, London, 1987.

12 Charles MacIntosh, *The Practical Gardener and Modern Horticulturalist*, Thos. Kelly, London. Vol. 1. 1830, p.3.

13 *Ibid*, p.9.

14 *Slip*: 'A strip, a narrow piece or stretch of land, ground etc'. First recorded in 1591. *Oxford English Dictionary*, Volume 9, 1961, p.216. In the context of kitchen gardens this refers to the narrow strip or strips of land outside the main enclosure. Such strips were usually enclosed by low walling.

15 Richard Bradley, *New Improvements of Planting and Gardening*, London, 1726, p.43.

16 Somerset County Record Office, DD/DB 7/13.

17 J.C. Loudon, *The Suburban Gardener and Villa Companion*, London, 1838, p.108.

18 Arthur W. Preston and John E.T. Pollard, *The History of the Norfolk and Norwich Horticultural Society 1829–1929*, Norwich, 1929, p.16.

19 Gervase Markham, *The Second Booke of the English Husbandman*, London, 1614, p.16.

Chapter 7 (pages 119–33)

1 Warwick Wroth, *The London Pleasure Gardens of the Eighteenth Century*, MacMillan, London, 1896, pp.93–110.

2 *Ibid.*, p.247.

3 *Ibid.*, p.77.

4 For example, Lord Cobham's Head (1728): *Ibid.*, p.68; Peerless Pool (1734); *Ibid.*, pp.81–5.

5 *Ibid.*, p.60.

6 'An Act for the Better Preventing Thefts and Robberies, and for Regulating Places of Public Entertainment, and Punishing Persons Keeping Disorderly Houses'. 'Publick Act', 1st June 1752. As described in *Statutes at Large from the Twentieth Year of the Reign of King George the Second to the Thirtieth Year of the Reign of King George the Second*, Volume 7, London, 1769, pp.438–40.

7 See, for example, Trevor Fawcett, 'The Norwich Pleasure Gardens', *Norfolk Archaeology* 35, 5 (1972) pp.382–99.

8 Warwick Wroth, *op.cit.*, p.131.

9 *Ibid.*, p.225.

10 *Ibid.*, p.266.

11 *Ibid.*, p.286.

12 William B. Boulton, *Amusements of Old London*, The Tabard Press, London, Vol. 2, 1970, p.124.

13 Warwick Wroth, *op.cit.*, p.189.

14 William B. Boulton, *op.cit.*, p.149.

15 *Ibid.*, p.135.

16 *Ibid.*, p.155.

18 George F. Chadwick, *The Park and the Town*, The Architectural Press, London, 1966, p.24.

19 Melanie L. Simo, 'John Claudius Loudon: On Planning and Design for the Garden Metropolis', *Garden History* 9, 2 (1981), pp.184–201, p.185.

20 *Gardeners Chronicle*, 24 April, 1841, p.259.

21 Chadwick, *op.cit.*, p.32.

22 *Ibid.*, p.138.

23 *Ibid.*, p.68.

24 *Ibid.*, p.71.

25 Wroth, *op.cit.*, p.137.

26 Fawcett, *op.cit.*, p.396.

27 Walter Wicks, *Inns and Taverns of Old Norwich with Notes on Pleasure Gardens*, Norwich, 1925, p.138.

28 Warwick Wroth, *op.cit.*, p.165.

29 Chadwick, *op.cit.*, pp.106–7.

30 See, for example: Melanie L. Simo, *op.cit.*, p.184, regarding the enclosure of Hampstead Heath.

31 Neil McMaster, 'The Battle for Mousehold Heath 1857–1884: "Popular Politics" and the Victorian Public Park', *Past and Present* 127 (1990), pp.117–54.

32 Chadwick, *op.cit.*, p.109.

33 *A Few Pages About Manchester*, Love & Barton, Manchester, *c.*1850, p.32.

34 W. Adam, *Gem of the Peak*, John & Charles Mozley, Derby, 1857.

35 J.C. Loudon, *Derby Arboretum*, London, 1840, p.95.

36 Mark Girouard, *The Victorian Country House*, Yale University Press, London, 1979, pp.205–12.

37 *Ibid.*, p.212.

38 For a discussion of the Acts for the Provision of Public Parks, see: George F. Chadwick, *op.cit.*, p.32.

39 Northallerton Record Office, MIC 1519.

40 A.R. Sennett, *Garden Cities in Theory and Practice*, Bemrose, London, 1905, p.25.

41 James Stevens Curl, 'The Architecture and Planning of the Nineteenth-Century Cemetery', *Garden History* 3, 3 (1975), pp.13–41; p.15.

42 George Alfred Walker, 'Gatherings From Graveyards', London, 1839.

43 J.C. Loudon, *On Laying Out Cemeteries*, Spottiswoode, London, 1843, p.21.

44 See, for example, James Stevens Curl, 'Loudon and the Garden Cemetery Movement', *Garden History* 11, 2 (1983), pp.133–56; and John Gay and Felix Barker, *Highgate Cemetery: Victorian Valhalla*. John Murray, London, 1986, p.15.

45 Nicholas Penny, 'The Macabre Garden at

Denbies and its Monument', *Garden History* 3, 3 (1975), pp.58–61.

46 Susanne Seymour, 'The Spirit of Planting', *The East Midlands Geographer* 12, 1 and 2 (1989), pp.5–13.

47 James Stevens Curl, 'The Architecture and Planning of the Nineteenth-Century Cemetery', p.19.

48 *Ibid.*, p.21.

49 *The Builder* 20 (1862), p.362.

50 James Stevens Curl, 'The Design of Early British Cemeteries', *Journal of Garden History* 4, 3 (1984), pp.223–56; p.245. Curl, 'The Architecture and Planning of the Nineteenth Century Cemetery', p.14, pp.29–33.

51 J.C. Loudon, *On Laying Out Cemeteries*, p.21.

52 *Ibid.*, p.20.

53 *Ibid.*, pp.68–9.

54 *Ibid.*, pp.95–115.

55 Robert Errington, 'On The Deodar', *Journal of the Horticultural Society*, 5 (1850), pp.111–13. Robert Errington was gardener to Sir Philip Malpas de Grey Egerton, at Oulton Park, near Tarporley (Cheshire).

56 J.C. Loudon, *On Laying out Cemeteries*, p.21.

57 *Ibid.*, pp.13 and 22.

58 *Ibid.*, p.39.

59 Nicholas Penny, 'The Commercial Garden Necropolis of the Early Nineteenth Century and its Critics', *Garden History* 2, 3 (1974), pp.61–76; pp.71–2.

60 John Gay and Felix Barker, *op.cit.*, pp.7–44.

Chapter 8 (pages 134–46)

1 See, for example, Heather A. Clemenson, *English Country Houses and Landed Estates*, Croom Helm, London, 1982.

2 Mark Girouard, *The Victorian Country House*, Yale University Press, London, 1979, pp.366–74.

3 *Gardens Old and New*. Country Life, London, n.d., *c.*1898, p.15.

4 *Ibid.*, pp.172–7.

5 *Ibid.*, p.15.

6 *Ibid.*, p.92.

7 A.R. Sennett, *Garden Cities in Theory and Practice*, Bemrose, London, 1905, p.3.

8 *Gardens Old and New*, p.242.

9 Phillada Ballard, '*Rus in Urbe*: Joseph Chamberlain's Gardens at Highbury, Moor Green, Birmingham, 1879–1914', *Garden History* 14, 1 (1986), pp.61–76.

10 Audrey Le Lievre, 'An Account of the Garden at Aldenham House and of its Makers: Henry Hucks Gibbs, Vicary Gibbs and Edwin Beckett', *Garden History* 14, 2 (1986), pp.173–93.

11 *Gardening Illustrated for Town and Country*, London, 16 Jan., 1886, p.653.

12 *Gardens Old and New*, p.228.

13 See, for example, Jane Brown, *Gardens of a Golden Afternoon*, Penguin Books, Harmondsworth, 1982, pp.182–3.

14 Walter P. Wright, *The Perfect Garden*, London, 1911.

15 Andrew Clayton-Payne and Brent Elliott, *Victorian Flower Gardens*, Weidenfeld & Nicolson, London, 1988, p.104.

16 *Ibid.*, p.142.

17 Forestry Commission Archives. Stanton Downham, Suffolk.

18 Watford Public Library, Hertfordshire.

19 See, for example, H. Prince, 'Parkland in the Chilterns', *Geographical Review* 49 (1959), p.31.

20 The Duchess of Devonshire, *The Garden at Chatsworth*, Derbyshire Countryside, Derby, 1987, p.32.

21 Alistair Forsyth, *Yesterdays Gardens*, Royal Commission on Historic Monuments, London, 1983, p.9, Illustration No. 11.

22 Audrey Le Lievre, *op.cit.*, pp.191–2.

23 Geoffrey Jellicoe, 'Ronald Tree and the Gardens of Ditchley Park: The Human face of History', *Garden History* 10, 1 (1982), pp.80–91.

24 Brochure for 'English Country Cottages', 1991.

25 *The Landmark Trust Handbook* 1987, with revisions 1991.

26 Ralph Dutton, *The English Garden*, Batsford, London 1937, p.7.

Index